NATIONAL ACTION PLAN

Priorities for Managing Freshwater Resources in a Changing Climate

Interagency Climate Change Adaptation Task Force

October 2011

Disclaimer

This National Action Plan reflects the current thinking of the Interagency Climate Change Adaptation Task Force regarding climate change and water resources. The Task Force reserves the right to modify the recommendations included in the document, or act in a manner different from this document as appropriate. The actions and recommendations included in this National Action Plan are judged to be both a high priority today and achievable in the context of existing and foreseeable agency capacity. This National Action Plan is not a final agency action subject to judicial review, nor is it considered a rule. Nothing in this Plan is meant to, or in fact does, affect the substantive or legal rights of third parties or bind the Federal agencies.

Contents

Rio de Los Angeles State Park, Los Angeles, California

Executive Summary

Freshwater resources are critical to the health of people, the environment, and the economy. Recent studies and assessments of climate change impacts, including the 2009 "Global Climate Change Impacts in the United States" prepared by the U.S. Global Change Research Program, identify several major impacts of a changing climate on the Nation's fresh-water resources. For instance, projected increases in air temperatures will lead to warmer waters. Rainfall amounts are expected to decline in some areas and increase in others, while the proportion of precipitation that falls as snow decreases. Rainfall and storms are expected to be more intense. In some

> "Of all the potential threats posed by climatic variability and change, those associated with water resources are arguably the most consequential for both society and the environment."
>
> Water—the Nation's Fundamental Climate Issue: A White Paper on the U.S. Geological Survey Role and Capabilities; U.S. Department of the Interior, U.S. Geological Survey, Circular 1347, 2010

areas rising sea level is projected to inundate water infrastructure, such as water treatment facilities, and degrade coastal groundwater resources.

These impacts of a changing climate pose significant challenges for managers of freshwater resources. Ensuring adequate water supply will be more difficult. New problems will arise for water managers working to protect human life, health, and property. Changing water-resources conditions will also make protecting the quality of freshwater resources, habitats, and aquatic life more complex.

In October 2010, the Interagency Climate Change Adaptation Task Force published a Progress Report to the President describing Federal agency actions needed to better prepare the Nation to respond to the impacts of a changing climate. The Progress Report directed the Task Force's Water Resources and Climate Change Adaptation Workgroup to lead the development of a national action plan to identify steps that Federal agencies can take to improve management of freshwater resources in a changing climate.

This National Action Plan is based on the latest science on climate risks to freshwater resources and establishes the following national goal:

> *Government agencies and citizens collaboratively manage freshwater resources in response to a changing climate in order to ensure adequate water supplies, to safeguard human life, health and property, and to protect water quality and aquatic ecosystems.*

To accomplish this goal, the Plan makes six priority recommendations that are described briefly below. Specific actions in support of these recommendations are summarized in Table 1; more detailed information is provided in Section 4 and Appendix B.

RECOMMENDATIONS

1. Establish a Planning Process to Adapt Water Resources Management to a Changing Climate

This National Action Plan is an initial step to respond to the challenges to freshwater resources posed by a changing climate. The recommendations and actions in this Plan, however, will need to be evaluated and updated regularly over time. In addition, a more formal organizational framework is needed to link the efforts of Federal agencies with those of State, Tribal, and local governments and other interested parties.

2. Improve Water Resources and Climate Change Information for Decision-Making

Current decisionmaking tools and policies for water resources management rely on historical water data to estimate future variations in water availability and quality. In a changing climate, however, water data used in decisionmaking tools needs to be complete and current. In addition, new insights from predictive models need to be applied to key decisions.

3. Strengthen Assessment of Vulnerability of Water Resources to Climate Change

Climate change impacts—including extreme weather events, sea level rise, shifting precipitation and runoff patterns, among others—are expected to significantly affect the water environment, water infrastructure, and the operations of water resources facilities. To effectively reduce risks from climate change, water resource managers need improved tools to assess the climate change vulnerabilities in their systems that are tailored to the specific type of facility and most critical management decisions.

4. Expand Water Use Efficiency

Climate change will further challenge water resources that are already under stress because of growing populations, contamination, and demands to meet diverse human and ecosystem needs. Making more efficient use of water can extend the availability of current supplies, reduce competition among sectors, save energy, and reduce the cost of water system operations.

5. Support Integrated Water Resources Management

Management of the risks from a changing climate should not occur in isolation and needs to be integrated with efforts to address other challenges to freshwater resources management. As models and methods for integrated water resources management are developed across the country, challenges posed by a changing climate need to be incorporated.

6. Support Training and Outreach to Build Response Capability

Today, the workforce that manages water resources programs at all levels of government and in the private sector needs information and tools to recognize the implications of a changing climate or to make complex climate change adaptation decisions related to freshwater resources.

The Task Force recognizes that managing the risks to freshwater resources posed by a changing climate is a complex and multifaceted undertaking for which many recommendations and actions might be appropriate. This National Action Plan presents recommendations and actions that are judged to be both a high priority today and achievable in the context of existing and foreseeable agency capacity. As described in more detail in Section 4, this document is an initial step in planning for climate change risks to freshwater resources that is expected to be evaluated, revised, and expanded in the years ahead.

Finally, this Plan is part of a larger set of climate change adaptation activities, including:

- **National Climate Assessment** The 2009 national climate assessment, published by the U.S. Global Change Research Program, includes an assessment of climate change impacts on water resources. The information published in that assessment provides the scientific foundation for this Plan. National assessments are required by law every four years and the next assessment in 2013 will provide new information about impacts, opportunities, and vulnerability as well as a basis for evaluating effectiveness of adaptation actions and determining next steps.

- **Federal Agency Climate Change Adaptation Planning** The 2010 Progress Report of the Climate Change Adaptation Task Force recommended that agencies integrate adaptation into their ongoing planning to ensure that resources are invested wisely and that Federal operations, policies and programs remain effective in a changing climate. Implementing instructions for this work were issued by the Council on Environmental Quality in March 2011 and include a requirement that agency-specific climate change adaptation plans be published by June 2012. This National Action Plan for freshwater resources will inform and guide development of water resources related elements of agency adaptation planning.

- **Other Natural Resources Strategies** In addition to calling for this freshwater action plan, the 2010 Progress Report supports the development of a national strategy to strengthen the resilience of coastal, ocean and Great Lakes ecosystems to climate change and ocean acidification and the development of a national climate adaptation strategy focused on fish, wildlife and plants. These three natural resource strategies have common elements and development of these strategies is being closely coordinated. For example, the strategy addressing fish, wildlife and plants, now being developed under the leadership of the U.S. Fish and Wildlife Service, the National Oceanic and Atmospheric Administration, and State fish and wildlife agencies, is addressing climate adaptation needs on an ecosystem basis (e.g., forests, grasslands, freshwater ecosystems) and will speak to actions for freshwater ecosystem adaptation in greater detail.

- **Existing Water Resources and Climate Change Adaptation Activities** Federal agencies, as well as State and local governments and others, are already implementing substantial efforts to adapt the management of water resources to a changing climate. The activities of Federal agencies are briefly discussed in Section 3 of this document and are described in more detail in Appendix C.

Table 1. Summary of Recommendations and Actions

Recommendation 1 Establish a Planning Process

Action 1   Establish a planning process with the capability to identify priority adaptation actions and promote their implementation

Action 2   Establish an organizational framework to promote effective management of water resources in a changing climate

Recommendation 2 Improve Water Resources and Climate Change Information for Decisionmaking

Action 3   Strengthen data for understanding climate change impacts on water resources

Action 4   Create a program to align "hydroclimatic" statistics with today's climate and anticipate future changes

Action 5   Implement surveillance system for tracking waterborne disease/health threats relevant to climate change

Action 6   Provide coastal states/communities with information to identify areas likely to be inundated by sea level rise

Action 7   Establish interagency effort to expedite implementation of the newly developed wetlands mapping standard

Recommendation 3 Strengthen Assessment of Vulnerability of Water Resources to Climate Change

Action 8   Publish guidance on the use of modeled projections for water resources applications

Action 9   Develop a Federal internet portal to provide information on water resources and climate change

Action 10   Develop a pilot climate change vulnerability index for a major category of water facilities

Action 11   Continue development of tools and approaches that build capacity for water institutions to conduct vulnerability assessments and implement appropriate responses

Action 12   Assess vulnerability of watersheds and aquatic systems in National Forests and Grasslands

Action 13   Promote free and open access to authoritative climate change science and water resources data

Recommendation 4 Expand Water Use Efficiency

Action 14   Develop nationally consistent metrics for water use efficiency in key sectors

Action 15   Consider making water use efficiency an explicit consideration in the revision of Principles and Standards for water resources projects and in the new NEPA guidance on climate change

Action 16   Enhance coordination among current Federal water efficiency programs and create a "toolbox" of key practices

Recommendation 5 Support Integrated Water Resources Management

Action 17   Work with States and interstate bodies (e.g., river basin commissions) to provide assistance needed to incorporate IWRM into their planning and programs, paying particular attention to climate change adaptation issues

Action 18   Revise Federal water project planning standards to address climate change

Action 19   Work with States to review flood risk management and drought management planning to identify "best practices" to prepare for hydrologic extremes

Action 20   Develop benchmarks for incorporating adaptive management into water project designs, operational procedures, and planning strategies

Recommendation 6 Support Training and Outreach to Build Response Capability

Action 21   Establish a core training program on climate change science for local, Tribal, and State water resources managers

Action 22   Focus existing youth outreach programs on climate change and water issues

Action 23   Engage Water Resources Research Institutes at land grant colleges in climate change adaptation research

Action 24   Increase graduate level fellowships in water management and climate change

Introduction

This National Action Plan provides an overview of the challenges that a changing climate presents for the management of the Nation's water resources and recommends actions for Federal agencies to support water resource managers in understanding and reducing the risks of climate change.

This Plan was developed in response to a recommendation in the October 2010 Progress Report of the Interagency Climate Change and Adaptation Task Force (referred to hereafter as the Task Force; see http://www.whitehouse.gov/administration/eop/ceq/initiatives/adaptation). It was developed for the Task Force by an interagency Water Resources and Climate Change Adaptation Workgroup (hereafter the Workgroup) made up of representatives from Federal agencies involved in water resources management. The Workgroup is co-chaired by the Department of Interior (DOI), the Environmental Protection Agency (EPA), and the Council on Environmental Quality (CEQ) (see Appendix A for a listing of Workgroup members).

> "Given the breadth of climate change impacts and corresponding adaptation measures, certain key climate related issues will require a collaborative approach from the Federal government, such as water resource management..."
>
> Progress Report of the Interagency Climate Change Adaptation Task Force: Recommended Actions in Support of a National Climate Change Adaptation Strategy; October 2010, p.34

Beginning in 2009, the Workgroup held "listening sessions" with organizations outside the Federal government, reviewed scientific literature relating to the impacts of climate change on water resources, and reviewed existing efforts by Federal agencies involved in water resources management to adapt to a changing climate.

Drawing on this analysis, the Workgroup identified key concepts and specific actions to support adaptation of water resources management to a changing climate. Some of this initial work was included in the water resources section of the October 2010 Progress Report.

This National Action Plan describes the major climate change risks to freshwater resources management and summarizes current Federal agency activities to reduce these risks. A summary of comments and suggestions received from organizations and individuals during public listening sessions is also provided in Appendix D.

Six recommendations to improve water resources management in a changing climate are presented in this Plan. For each of these recommendations, the Plan identifies specific actions that Federal agencies should consider to reduce climate risks to freshwater resources. A table summarizing recommendations and supporting actions is provided in Appendix B.

The October 2010 Progress Report of the Climate Change Adaptation Task Force also supported the development of a national climate adaptation strategy focused on fish, wildlife and plants and a national strategy to strengthen the resilience and adaptability of coastal, ocean, and Great Lakes ecosystems to climate change and ocean acidification. These three natural resources strategies share common elements and development of these plans is being coordinated.

1

Water Resources Management Challenges Posed by a Changing Climate

Water resources are managed by Federal, State, Tribal, and local governments with a wide range of objectives. Some of the key challenges that a changing climate poses for these efforts are described in this section.

Overview of Climate Change Impacts on Water Resources

To understand the challenges that water resources managers face in adapting to a changing climate, it is useful to understand some of the impacts that climate change may have on water resources. Some of the primary climate change risks for water resources are described below. These impacts may occur individually or cumulatively at specific locations.

Air and Water Temperature Increases

Warmer air and water temperatures will have significant impacts on water resources and aquatic habitats, including shifts in aquatic species distribution and population, increased concentrations of some pollutants, and increased eutrophication in some water bodies. The U.S. Global Change Research Program (USGCRP) concluded that "All climate models project that human-caused emissions of heat-trapping gases will cause further warming in the future...global average temperature is projected to rise by 2 to 11.5°F by the end of this century (relative to the 1980-1999 time period)" (U.S. Global Change Research Program, 2009, p. 24).

"Climate change has already altered, and will continue to alter, the water cycle, affecting where, when, and how much water is available for all uses."

Global Climate Change Impacts in the United Sates, 2009

More specifically, the USGCRP finds that by 2100, the average U.S. temperature is projected to increase by approximately 4 to 6.5°F under the lower emissions scenario and by approximately 7 to 11°F under the higher emissions scenario (U.S. Global Change Research Program, 2009, p. 29). Climate models project regional variation of warming (e.g., some models project that temperatures in parts of Alaska could increase by 18°F). Water temperatures have been rising and increases have been observed in both saltwater and freshwater (U.S. Global Change Research Program, 2009, p. 390; Kaushal et al., 2010, p. 5).

Changes in Amounts and Distribution of Rainfall and Snowfall

As the climate warms, some areas will receive more precipitation while others will receive less, particularly in the western United States.

In addition, warmer temperatures will shift the form of precipitation from snow to rain and also result in earlier melting of snowpacks. These changes are expected to lead to decreases in the size of snowpacks and bring about earlier runoff in areas where seasonal cycles of runoff have historically been dominated by snowmelt. Such changes have already been documented in some areas of western North America (Knowles et al., 2006). This loss of snowpack storage is expected to result in a decrease in the amount of reliable water supply in areas where snow has been a major component of the hydrologic system.

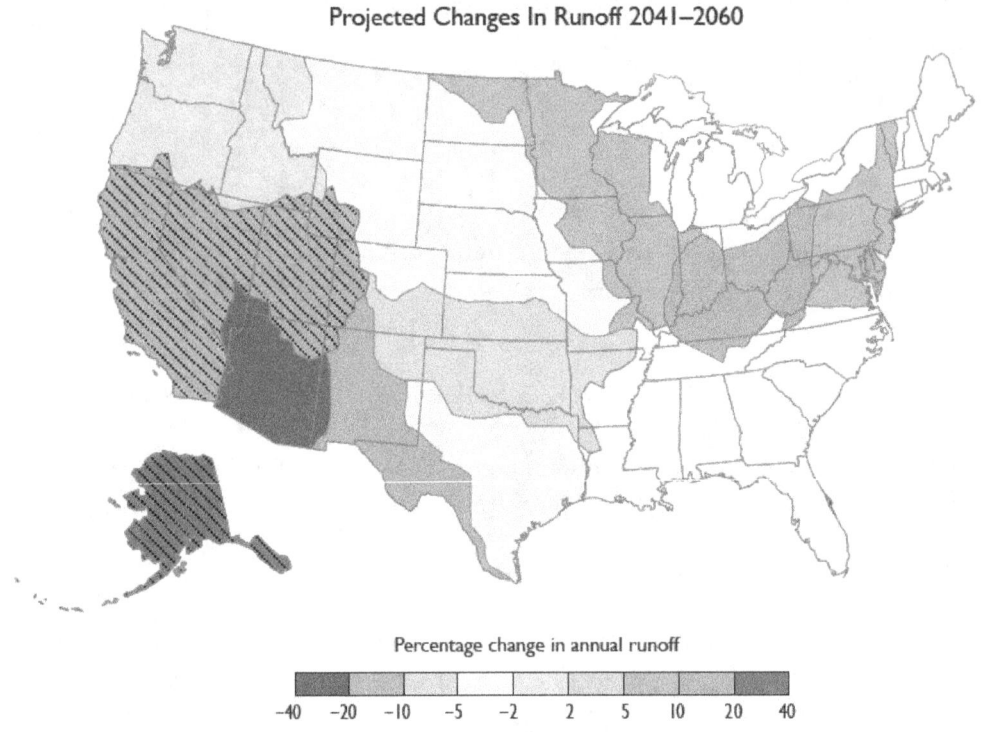

Projected Changes In Runoff 2041–2060

Percentage change in annual runoff

−40   −20   −10   −5   −2   2   5   10   20   40

Modified from Milly et al., 2008

Runoff, which accumulates as streamflow, is the amount of precipitation that is not evaporated, stored as snowpack or soil moisture, or filtered down to groundwater. Projected changes in median runoff for 2041–2060, relative to a 1901–1970 baseline, are mapped by water-resource region. Colors indicated percentage changes in runoff. Hatched areas indicate greater confidence due to strong agreement among model projections. White areas indicate divergence among model projections. Results are based on emissions in between the lower and higher emission scenarios.

Over the past 50 years, precipitation has increased an average of about 5 percent across the nation (U.S. Global Change Research Program, 2009, p. 30). In addition, projections of future precipitation generally indicate that northern areas will become wetter and southern areas, especially in the West, will become drier (U.S. Global Change Research Program, 2009, p. 30).

USGCRP also indicated that "Over the last 50 years, there have been widespread temperature related reductions in snowpack in the West, with the largest reductions occurring in lower elevation mountains in the Northwest and California, where snowfall occurs at temperatures close to the freezing point. The Northeast has also experienced snowpack reductions during a similar period. Observations indicate a transition to more rain and less snow in both the West and Northeast in the last 50 years" (U.S. Global Change Research Program, 2009, p. 45). The Intergovernmental Panel on Climate Change (IPCC) also concluded that "Snow season length and snow depth are very likely to decrease in most of North America" (Christensen et al. 2007, p. 887).

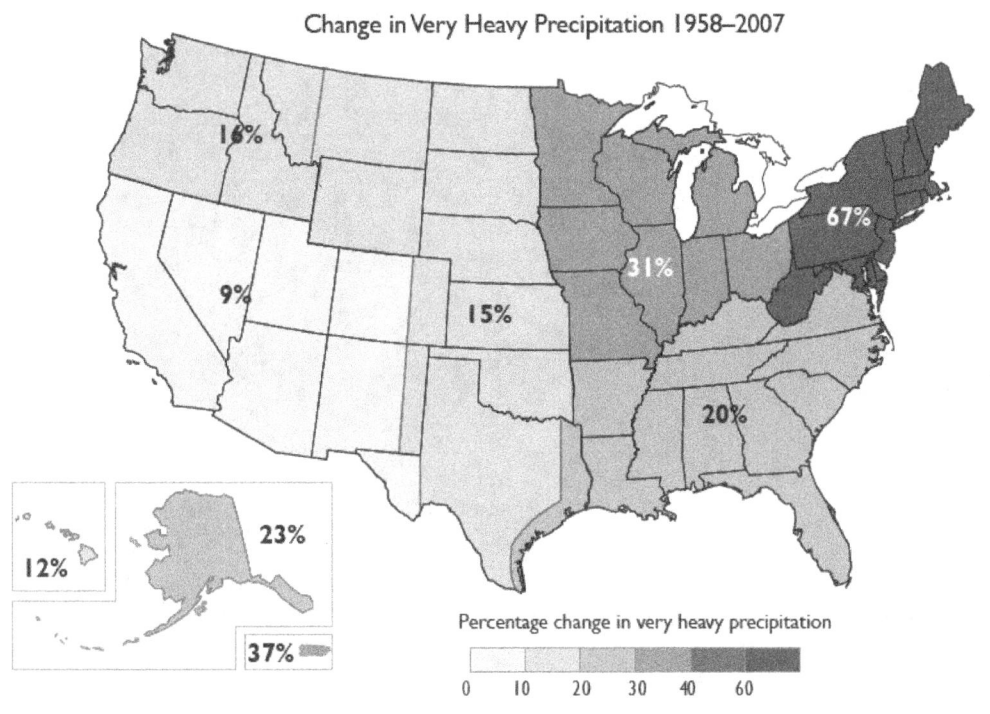

Percentage increases in the amount falling in very heavy precipitation events (defined as the heaviest 1% of all daily events) from 1958–2007 for each region.

Increased Intensity of Rainfall and Storms

As the climate warms, the hydrologic system becomes more dynamic, the intensity of storms increases and rainfall occurs more often as a downpour. The USGCRP reports that "The amount of rain falling in the heaviest downpours has increased approximately 20 percent on average, in the past century, and this trend is very likely to continue, with the largest increases in the wettest places" (U.S. Global Change Research Program, 2009, p. 32). In addition, climate models project continued increases in the frequency and intensity of the heaviest downpours during this century (ibid). For example, heavy downpours that are now 1-in-20-year occurrences are projected to occur about every 4 to 15 years by the end of this century, depending on location, and the intensity of heavy downpours is also expected to increase. The 1-in-20-year heavy downpour is expected to be between 10 and 25 percent heavier by the end of the century than it is now (ibid).

The USGCRP also finds that "As ocean temperatures continue to increase in the future, it is likely that hurricane rainfall and wind speeds will increase in response to human-caused warming. Analyses of model simulations suggest that for each 1.8°F (1°C) increase in tropical sea surface temperatures, core rainfall rates will increase by 6 to 18 percent and the surface wind speeds of the strongest hurricanes will increase by about 1 to 8 percent. Even without additional coastal development, hurricane damages and storm surge levels and hurricane damages are likely to increase because of increasing hurricane intensity coupled with sea-level rise, the latter being a virtually certain outcome of the warming global climate." (U.S. Global Change Research Program, 2009, p. 36).

Infrastructure At Risk From Sea Level Rise

Source: US Global Change Research Program, 2009

Sea Level Rise

Rising sea levels resulting from a warming climate are likely to cause a complex set of interrelated impacts on coastal freshwater aquifers and the threat of inundation to water-related infrastructure (e.g., sewage treatment plants and drinking-water treatment plants).

The USGCRP indicates that "After at least 2,000 years of little change, sea level rose by roughly 8 inches over the past century. Satellite data available over the past 15 years show sea level rising at a rate roughly double the rate observed over the past century." (U.S. Global Change Research Program, 2009, p. 18). The report also states "…assuming historical geological forces continue, a 2-foot rise in global sea level (which is within the range of recent estimates) by the end of this century would result in a relative sea-level rise of 2.3 feet at New York City, 2.9 feet at Hampton Roads, Virginia, 3.5 feet at Galveston, Texas, and 1 foot at Neah Bay in Washington state." (U.S. Global Change Research Program, 2009, p. 37).

Recent observations confirm that trend; a 2011 study shows that the melting of the Antarctic and Greenland ice sheets is accelerating (Rignot, et al. 2011, p. 4). The researchers found that if these accelerating rates continue, global sea level rise could be as much as 1 foot within the next 40 years (National Aeronautics and Space Administration, 2011).

Indirect Impacts

It is likely that climate change mitigation actions will lead to adoption of low carbon fuel and energy technologies. Some of these technologies may have indirect impacts on water resources. For example, production of biofuels can result in increased competition for water supplies.

Climate Change Challenges for Water Resources Managers

The impacts of a changing climate are expected to pose significant challenges for water resources managers in three major areas: ensuring adequate water supply; protecting human life, health, and property; and protecting the quality of freshwater resources.

These challenges for water resources managers are interconnected in many ways and are not presented here in any particular order. Some of the key elements of these major challenges are summarized below.

Ensuring Adequate Water Supplies

Ensuring adequate supplies of freshwater, including surface water and groundwater, needed to support key sectors, including:

- municipal drinking water supplies;
- navigation, recreation, and tourism;
- agriculture;
- energy development, production, and generation (including hydropower, fossil fuels, and biofuels);
- industry; and
- aquatic ecosystems and ecosystem services.

The reliability of water supplies for these sectors is in question as a result of anticipated reductions in precipitation in some regions of the country as well as earlier runoff of snowmelt. Other examples of climate-change-related factors influencing the reliability of water supplies include increases in forest fire damage in watersheds that are sources of supply and impairment of freshwater supplies from salt-water intrusion resulting from sea level rise.

Protecting Human Life, Health, and Property

Protecting human life, health, and property at increased risk from the impacts of a warmer climate on freshwater resources, including risks associated with:

- increased water-borne and vector-borne disease;
- increased difficulty in treating drinking water (e.g., due to increased turbidity of waters);
- increased flooding in some areas as the hydrologic system becomes more variable;
- increased drought and wildfires in some areas; and
- disruptions of power, water, sewer, and emergency services as a result of more extreme rainfall and storms.

These increased risks to life, health, and property can be traced to changes in freshwater resource conditions that result from a changing climate, including a linkage between heavy precipitation and disease outbreaks, changes in rainfall levels and watershed resilience that make floods more severe, and increases in extreme weather events that disrupt power, water and emergency services.

"Some of the most important societal and ecological impacts anticipated in this region [i.e., North America] stem from changes in surface and groundwater hydrology."

Intergovernmental Panel on Climate Change, 2008

Protecting the Quality of Freshwater Resources

Protecting the quality of freshwater resources throughout the country, including:

- the quality of surface water and groundwater;
- the health of fisheries and aquatic habitat; and
- wetlands needed for sustainable aquatic ecosystems.

Examples of the connections between changing climatic conditions and the quality of freshwater include more challenging water treatment as a result of higher concentrations of contaminants in receiving waters and more variable streamflows, more difficult management of stormwater because of more intense rainfall patterns, and changes in aquatic-system characteristics allowing invasive species to become more widely established.

Photo courtesy of the National Oceanic and Atmospheric Administration

2

Current Federal Agency Activities to Manage Climate Change Risks to Water Resources

The Water Resources and Climate Change Adaptation Workgroup reviewed the broad range of activities underway throughout the Federal government, within individual agencies as well as in cooperative interagency projects (see Appendix C). Although not exhaustive, this review illustrates the breadth and depth of ongoing activities to address climate change impacts on water resources.

Conclusions from Workgroup Review

On the basis of this review of agency activities, the Workgroup came to the following conclusions:

Agencies are taking significant steps to reduce climate risks to freshwater resources

Federal agencies are making significant efforts to respond to the three major challenges that a changing climate poses for water resources identified in Section 1. For example, the Army Corps of Engineers (USACE) developed guidance for including sea level change in project planning, the Environmental Protection Agency (EPA) developed a water utility climate change vulnerability assessment tool, and the Bureau of Reclamation (USBR) developed new science and pursued studies to understand climate impacts on western water basins. In addition, several major studies of climate change and water resources required by the Omnibus Public Lands Act are nearing completion or have recently been provided to Congress (see box).

> **Water Resources and Climate Change Studies: Omnibus Public Lands Act**
>
> **Section 9503** Impacts of climate change on water in USBR reclamation basins
>
> **Section 9505** Impacts of climate change on hydroelectric power
>
> **Section 9506** Water data and information needed for climate change adaptation
>
> **Section 9507** Location and extent of brackish groundwater
>
> **Section 9508** Assessment of current water shortages

Federal agencies are also in the process of developing agency-specific climate change adaptation plans by June 2012 in accordance with instructions issued by the Council on Environmental Quality (CEQ) in March 2011. These plans are intended to help agencies integrate adaptation into their ongoing planning to ensure that resources are invested wisely and that Federal operations, policies and programs remain effective in a changing climate.

Cooperative efforts for climate change adaptation of freshwater resources management are valuable

Federal agencies have initiated interagency projects to address the impacts of a changing climate on water resources. These projects are making valuable contributions to understanding and responding to a changing climate. For example, the Department of the Interior (DOI) has begun to establish 8 regional Climate Science Centers (CSCs) and is creating 21 Landscape Conservation Cooperatives (LCCs). In addition, Federal agencies have been working closely with the governments of Mexico and Canada through existing institutional arrangements to ensure that climate adaptation planning is included in management of shared waters.

**Existing Federal efforts to reduce climate risks to freshwater resources
need to be strengthened and sustained**

Significant work to help adapt water resources to a changing climate has been undertaken by Federal agencies to date, (e.g., DOI's LCCs and CSCs, National Oceanic and Atmospheric Administration's (NOAA) Regional Integrated Sciences and Assessments (RISAs), Army Corps of Engineers guidance on accounting for sea level rise, and EPA and Forest Service planning for climate change). These efforts, however, need to be strengthened and sustained to address the extensive and complex challenges that water managers face from a changing climate.

**A national forum to coordinate efforts to reduce climate change risks
to freshwater resources is lacking**

Although cases of valuable interagency cooperative actions exist (e.g., the Climate Change and Water Working Group (CCAWWG), the DOI/Department of Commerce (DOC) Memorandum of Understanding on climate change, and the Floodplain Management Task Force), there does not presently exist a national forum for fostering communication and coordination for work related to climate change and water resources adaptation among the full range of relevant Federal agencies.

**A strategic approach for Federal agency action to reduce risks to freshwater
from climate change is needed**

Both the agency-specific projects and the cooperative projects described in Appendix C were developed in the absence of an overall, interagency strategy for prioritizing those actions Federal agencies could undertake to address water resources and climate change challenges that are the most timely and effective. Some important emerging examples of efforts that can form the foundation for the development of an interagency approach include the LCCs and the CCAWWG.

Better coordination with State and local adaptation efforts is needed

Efforts by Federal agencies to establish strong working relationships with States on common challenges, such as the Western States Federal Agency Support Team (WestFAST), show promise. In addition, the development by DOI of CSCs and LCCs, and RISAs by NOAA is expected to strengthen intergovernmental coordination on a wide range of climate change adaptation challenges, including challenges to water resources management. Furthermore, there is evidence of growing Federal, State, Tribal, and local coordination in some regions and locales that are excellent examples of collaboration to address targeted problems.

Photo courtesy of the National Oceanic and Atmospheric Administration

3
Public Comments

Input from the public was critical in the development of this National Action Plan. Given the broad and diverse array of stakeholders with interests in freshwater resources management, successful implementation of the Plan will depend on the applicability of recommendations and actions to stakeholder needs. The Workgroup created multiple avenues to collaborate with and receive feedback from the public in the development of the Plan. Stakeholder and public outreach activities and input are described in more detail in Appendix D.

Incorporating Public Input and Feedback

Public input and feedback to the Plan were solicited through three major mechanisms:

- a series of listening sessions with diverse stakeholders in the fall of 2009 to hear views and ideas about the general topic of water resources management and guide initial research and organization;
- a six-week public comment period on the draft Plan, including receipt of comments on a website designed for this purpose; and
- a second series of listening sessions with stakeholder organizations in mid 2011 to hear comments and suggestions on the draft Plan as released for public comment.

Overall, stakeholder and public reception to the draft Plan was positive. Feedback from both the listening sessions and written comments offered a valuable resource to the Workgroup and ensured that the final Plan reflected the perspectives, experiences, and concerns of interested organizations and individuals. Many of the commenters provided tangible examples of successful local, State, and regional policies and programs related to water resources management in the face of a changing climate. These helped strengthen the document.

Listening Sessions

Listening sessions were conducted in 2009 and 2011 with a range of stakeholder groups including:
- energy and industrial organizations;
- State, Tribal, and local governments;
- water utility organizations;
- environmental and coastal organizations;
- agriculture and transportation organizations; and
- public health organizations.

A number of consistent themes emerged throughout the public comment period and the Workgroup addressed these ideas in the final Plan to the extent possible.

Support for strengthening existing collaborative planning efforts

Many commenters supported the Plan's focus on strengthening collaborative structures among the community of Federal agencies, State, Tribal, and local governments, river basin commissions, non-governmental organizations, and the research community rather than establish major new organizations or programs.

Strengthen infrastructure planning for changing extremes

Comments received in the review of the draft Plan encouraged greater recognition of the importance of improved planning for water infrastructure. Several commenters recommended that the Plan also give greater attention to expanded use of "green infrastructure" practices. Other commenters recommended expanded attention to the value and operations of dams to better manage increasingly variable water resources.

Improve understanding of climate change impacts on aquatic ecosystems and watersheds

Many of the tools and collaborations being developed are focused on protection of infrastructure or water supply. Commenters indicated that more attention needs to be paid to understanding the effects of climate change on natural systems and developing strategies for improving their resilience.

Affirm the principle of integrated water resources management (IWRM)

Many commenters affirmed the Plan's recommendation to address climate and water challenges in the context of IWRM. IWRM, many participants agreed, is a critical organizing principle for managing scarce and fluctuating water resources across many sectors and users.

Expand Federal support for State, Tribal, and local climate adaptation

Commenters stressed the importance of water data and information, including reliable predictive models of future conditions, to support effective State and local adaptation decisions. In addition, many States, Tribes, regions, and localities are already implementing their own adaptation planning processes and Federal efforts toward managing freshwater resources in a changing climate should include expanded efforts to partner with, learn from, and help improve these activities, especially those related to climate change education.

Concern over sufficiency of recommended response actions in the context of challenges

Some commenters expressed concern that the proposed recommendations and supporting actions were needed but not sufficient to accomplish a significant shift in methods and approaches to water resources management suggested by projected changes in climate and water resources.

Protect indigenous communities

The Workgroup also heard from representatives of Tribal nations that indigenous people are subject to a range of challenges related to a changing climate. Many of these communities have observed climate-related changes that are already underway. Listening-session participants stressed that these effects are not simply "changes" to be adapted to—they represent a fundamental crisis of survival for communities' livelihoods and cultures.

Priority Recommendations for Reducing Climate Change Risks to Freshwater Resources

This National Action Plan establishes a goal for managing freshwater resources in a changing climate, identifies 6 key recommendations to achieve that goal, and describes 24 specific supporting actions that Federal agencies should take to implement the recommendations over the next several years.

Overall Goal and Priority Recommendations

Using input from listening sessions and considering information on scientific and Federal programs, the Task Force is adopting the following goal for managing freshwater resources in a changing climate:

Government agencies and citizens collaboratively manage freshwater resources in response to a changing climate in order to ensure adequate water supplies, to protect human life, health and property, and to protect water quality and aquatic ecosystems.

Specific recommendations supporting this goal are:

1. **Establish a Planning Process to Adapt Water Resources Management to a Changing Climate** (including continuing interagency coordination and expanding outreach to, and collaboration with, State, Tribal, and local governments and other stakeholders);

2. **Improve Water Resources and Climate Change Information for Decisionmaking** (including observational data, predictive models, measures of progress, and regular updates of analyses);

3. **Strengthen Assessment of Vulnerability of Water Resources to Climate Change** (including effective communication of data and development of risk assessment tools at multiple scales);

4. **Expand Water Use Efficiency** (including opportunities to develop water efficient technologies and to promote greater efficiency of water use and reuse);

5. **Support Integrated Water Resources Management** (including methods to promote resilience of water resources as the climate and environment changes); and

6. **Support Training and Outreach to Build Response Capability** (including practices to "mainstream" climate change adaptation into existing programs).

Specific supporting actions that Federal agencies should take to accomplish each recommendation are described below. For each supporting action, information concerning the lead Federal agency for that action and the implementation status of the action is provided in an adjoining text box. Implementation status described as "ready for implementation now" indicates that a lead agency has been identified and that the action can be accomplished within current resources or policies. "Requiring further development" indicates that additional work will need to be done in the next several years before the action can be deployed. A table summarizing recommendations and supporting actions is provided in Appendix B. This Appendix also indicates how the actions support the policy goals and supporting recommended actions identified in the October 2010 Progress Report of the Interagency Climate Change Adaptation Task Force. It is important to note that the proposal of an action in this report and the association of an action with a "lead agency" do not commit an agency to provide or seek funding for the action or to make related policy or program changes.

Implementation actions related to some of the six priority recommendations are already underway. For example, the October 2010 Progress Report highlighted the need to address water resource data issues and support more efficient use of water. Federal agencies are now working on these efforts. In the area of water data and information, Federal agencies have developed a report to Congress identifying a range of needed actions as required by Section 9506 of the Omnibus Public Lands Act.

Finally, the Task Force recognizes that managing the risks to freshwater resources posed by a changing climate is a complex and multi-faceted undertaking for which many recommendations and actions might be appropriate. This National Action Plan presents the recommendations and actions that are judged to be both a high priority today and achievable in the context of existing and foreseeable agency capacity. As described below, this document is an initial step in planning for climate change risks to freshwater resources and is expected to be evaluated, revised, and expanded in the years ahead.

Recommendation 1
Establish a planning process to adapt water resources management to a changing climate

A consistent theme at listening sessions and in discussions with Federal agency water resources program managers is the need for a clearly defined planning process and organizational framework for addressing water resources and climate change issues. Some of the key attributes of an effective planning process and organizational framework identified in these discussions are:

Involve State, Tribal, and local governments
An organizational framework for water resources adaptation to climate change needs to provide a material role for States, Tribes, and local governments and support collaboration with the governments of Canada and Mexico.

Prioritize the major challenges climate change poses for water resources
The organizational framework needs to support a planning process capable of setting priorities among the full range of Federal water resources challenges posed by climate change and should support agencies at different governmental levels in making informed choices about where to focus attention. Priority setting should reflect input from diverse stakeholders and be linked to Federal budgets and funding decisions.

Consider implications of adapting to impacts of climate change on resources other than water
Governments will increasingly be planning to manage the risks from the impacts of climate change on a range of resources other than water resources (e.g., energy, human health, soil resources, agriculture, forestry, fisheries, ecosystems, nonwater infrastructure). It is important that climate change adaptation be coordinated across these topics including plans to reduce greenhouse gas emissions. To date, planning for emissions reduction (i.e., mitigation) has largely overshadowed planning for managing the risks of a changing climate. Many of the practices that reduce greenhouse gases

(e.g., hydropower operations and development, bioenergy development, seeking access to natural gas reserves, sequestering carbon geologically or through land management or wetland protection practices) have potentially significant implications for water resources.

Consider other water resources challenges

An organizational framework should account for other significant challenges to sustainable water resources management that exist apart from climate change. Some of the major challenges include: expanding populations in many areas; depletion of aquifers in some areas and saltwater intrusion into aquifers in coastal areas; nutrient enrichment of rivers, lakes, reservoirs, and estuaries; aging infrastructure for storing and delivering water to users, for treating waste water, for navigation, for hydropower production, and for flood protection; emerging contaminants in groundwater and surface water that threaten human health and aquatic species; and the need for water to support the protection and restoration of aquatic ecosystems.

Build on existing institutional mechanisms

Existing organizational structures for coordination among water resource management agencies, the research community, and with public organizations involved in water resource management can play an important role in adapting water resources management to a changing climate. These existing mechanisms are described below and include the Subcommittee on Water Availability and Quality (SWAQ), the Advisory Committee on Water Information (ACWI) and the Climate Change and Water Working Group (CCAWWG). In addition, existing institutional capability for addressing climate change adaptation issues at a regional level (i.e., RISAs, CSCs and LCCs) should be actively engaged in addressing water resource issues.

Coordinate with research communities

The research community needs clear guidance on the information that is needed by decision-makers and planners to address adaptation challenges. In January 2011, the CCAWWG published "Addressing Climate Change in Long-Term Water Resources Planning and Management: User Needs for Improving Tools and Information" (U.S. Bureau of Reclamation, 2011). Other sectors of the water management communities have also recently published reports documenting their research needs, including the Western States Water Council, Water Utilities Climate Alliance, and Water Research Foundation. Today, the challenge is for the research community to develop strategies to respond to these needs in a coordinated and effective fashion.

Supporting Actions

The following specific actions support this recommendation.

1. Establish a planning process with the capability to identify priority adaptation actions and promote their implementation.

The development of this Plan is an important step in building the capability to manage freshwater resources in a changing climate. The Plan, however, will need to be revised over time as conditions change and as information on the effectiveness of the Plan becomes available. For this process to be successful, a timeline of major planning and evaluation actions is needed.

A key mechanism for understanding changing impacts of climate on water resources over time is the assessment prepared by the U.S. Global Change

Lead Agency:
Water Resources and Climate Adaptation Workgroup co-chairs (DOI/EPA/CEQ)

Implementation Status:
Now, with phase-in over coming years

Research Program. This comprehensive assessment of climate change impacts was last completed in 2009 and includes a section on water resources. Although the assessment process is now a continuing effort, a comprehensive report is required by law every 4 years. The next assessment report is planned for completion in 2013 (see box below).

Given the 4-year revision cycle for the national assessment, an appropriate time to revise the freshwater adaptation plan is two years after publication of the assessment (i.e., 2011 and 2015). This schedule allows for development of plan revisions based on full consideration of the most recent assessments.

A related consideration is that the natural resource strategies related to coasts, oceans and the Great Lakes and to fish, wildlife, and plants have elements in common with freshwater resources and these planning efforts need to be closely coordinated.

An important element of the water resources and climate change planning process is sustained evaluation of implementation actions and of the overall success of adaptation efforts.

This process should include:

- development of evaluation measures to track progress in improving adaptation of water resources to a changing climate, including both measures of program performance (e.g., timely development of plans or other actions) and outcome measures addressing overall success in supporting effective adaptation of water resources to climate change (e.g., as reflected in a periodic survey of water resource managers to request a self-assessment of adaptation progress);

Water Resources and Climate Change Planning Timeline

2009 National Climate Assessment
2011 Freshwater National Action Plan
2012 National Ocean Council Strategic Action Plan; National Fish, Wildlife, and Plants Climate Adaptation Strategy
2013 National Climate Assessment
2014 Independent Evaluation of Freshwater National Action Plan
2015 Revised Freshwater Action Plan

- publication of annual reports describing in narrative terms the progress being made toward overall goals and reporting on progress under each of the recommendations and supporting actions; and
- an evaluation in the third year of each 4-year planning cycle by an independent organization, such as the National Academy of Science or the National Academy of Public Administration, that provides an objective evaluation of the overall response of water resource managers to risks from a changing climate.

2. Establish an organizational framework to promote effective management of water resources in a changing climate.

An effective organizational framework to promote water resources adaptation to climate change includes four elements:

- Federal agency coordination;
- linkage to science and research;
- engagement in different regions of the country with State, local and Tribal governments; and
- participation of stakeholders and the public.

Lead Agency:
Workgroup chairs
(EPA/DOI/CEQ)

Implementation Status:
Now

The existing interagency Water Resources and Climate Change Adaptation Workgroup should be charged with continuing to support the Interagency Climate Change Adaptation Task Force in matters relating to freshwater resources. Section 16 of the Executive Order on Federal leadership on environmental, energy and economic performance (E.O. 13514) directs Federal agencies to "participate actively" in the work of the Task Force. Key objectives of the Workgroup should be to:

- foster Federal agency coordination at the national level on program management issues related to domestic freshwater and climate change, including oversight and coordination of existing water and climate activities;
- facilitate coordination among Federal water resource management agencies as they develop and implement water related elements of agency-specific climate change adaptation plans called for in the October 2010 Task Force Progress Report;
- manage development of plans and reports, including this National Action Plan for freshwater resources and the report to Congress on water data and information for climate change;
- cooperate and share "lessons learned" with State, Tribal, and local governments and organizations interested in water and climate change issues, including groups such as the Western Governors' Association, the Water Utility Climate Alliance, and other key organizations;
- coordinate with interagency teams developing climate change adaptation strategies related to coastal, ocean, and Great Lakes issues and to fish, wildlife and plant issues;
- oversee implementation of the recommendations and actions described in this National Action Plan; and
- work toward regional coordination of climate science and services being implemented in response to a recommendation for this effort in the October 2010 Progress Report of the Climate Change Adaptation Task Force.

To ensure effective coordination on science and research issues related to water resources and climate change, the existing Subcommittee on Water Availability and Quality (SWAQ), a subcommittee of the Committee on Environmental and Natural Resources and Sustainability (CENRS), should be charged with defining climate change and water research needs and identifying scientific issues. The SWAQ has made important contributions to scientific understanding of water resource issues and disseminating water resources research across Federal agencies. Adding climate change issues to the SWAQ's water resources research coordination charge will help integrate climate change research needs into the larger water research agenda. Likewise, the CCAWWG includes substantial scientific and technical expertise. The SWAQ, CCAWWG, and the Water Resources and Climate Change Adaptation Workgroup should actively cooperate and meet on a regular basis.

In addition, at present, there is no forum for climate modelers and managers of water data systems to resolve issues and differing interpretations in order to provide better clarity for end-users of information. Several Federal agencies presently fund the Water and Science Technology Board (WSTB) of the National Academies' National Research Council (NRC) to support a "standing committee" on issues related to hydrology. The US Global Change Research Program has also recently contracted with the NRC to provide a "one-stop shop" for guidance on global change research. This new institutional structure will ensure appropriate linkage across the various committees of the NRC, including the WSTB's committees. Federal agencies should continue to work with the NRC to ensure that the WSTB committee on hydrology is coordinated with the global change committee and others, as appropriate. They should pay particular attention to facilitating communication among water observational data managers and climate model experts to help resolve methodological differences and better tailor observational data to calibrate and verify model results.

A third element of a water and climate change adaptation organizational structure is effective engagement with Federal, State and local governments at the regional level. Climate change impacts, especially water-resources-related impacts, vary across the country. Several Federal agencies have established regional entities addressing climate change, including the Department of Interior CSCs, LCCs and the National Oceanic and Atmospheric Administration RISAs. The Interagency Climate Change Adaptation Task Force is working to strengthen networks of climate-related programs to deliver climate science and services efficiently and effectively in regions across the country. Federal agency water resources program managers should participate in these regional collaborations and reach out to stakeholders at the regional level.

> Water managers should take the initiative to clearly communicate their needs for applied science to the climate research community, and must seek opportunities to guide hydroclimatic research in directions that will support real world problem-solving.
>
> Western Governors' Association, 2008

Finally, it is essential that stakeholder organizations and the public are able to provide input as adaptation actions for climate change and water resources are planned and implemented. The Advisory Committee on Water Information (ACWI) is an existing public advisory group chartered under the Federal Advisory Committee Act (FACA) to advise the Federal government on water issues. The Committee is managed by the Department of the Interior and advises a range of Federal agencies on water matters. ACWI includes a variety of stakeholders with interests in water management, including States, Tribes, and other water related interest groups (see www.doi.acwi.gov). ACWI operates through an extensive subcommittee structure but does not currently have a subcommittee addressing issues relating to climate change. ACWI should consider options for how best to engage climate change and water issues, including establishing a new subgroup to help Federal agencies seek input and guidance from stakeholders and the public on climate and water issues or amending the charter and membership of an existing subgroup as needed to serve this purpose.

Recommendation 2
Improve water resources and climate change information for decisionmaking

Every day, all across the Nation, decisions are being made about water in both the public and private sectors. These decisions involve:

- supplying water for public drinking water systems, irrigation, electricity generation and transportation fuels production, or industrial activities;
- collecting and treating drinking water, wastewater and stormwater;
- developing new or alternative sources of water;
- protecting or restoring water bodies, aquatic habitats, and aquifers; or
- protecting citizens and infrastructure from the consequences of impaired water quality, extreme weather, flooding, and drought.

> "In a non-stationary world, continuity of observations is crucial."
>
> Milly et al., 2008

These water resources decisions, and the data systems needed to support them, are summarized in the Table in Appendix E. Analytic approaches currently exist for every one of these types of decisions. However, most of the current decisionmaking approaches rely on historical data to estimate future variations in water availability and quality.

Many decisions are based on hydro-climatic characteristics such as the mean flow of a river, the 50-year 1-hour rainfall intensity, the 7-day 10-year low flow, the "100-year" flood, or the mean August water temperature. These are estimated based on conditions of the past, but form the basis for design, investment, and water-allocation decisions that can have long-range (50–100 years) implications. Similarly, traditional methods for water system design and operation assume that what will happen hydrologically in the coming days, weeks, months, and years, can be estimated in a probabilistic sense from what we know of the current state of the watershed and records of past experience.

> "Extreme weather is influenced by climate change, and extreme weather events are now subject to human influence. The continued delay in taking action means we face rapidly worsening impacts, and unavoidable adaptation."
>
> Peter H. Gleick, Pacific Institute

In response to the requirements of Section 9506 of the Omnibus Public Lands Act, an interagency group worked over the past year to prepare a report on the technical challenges related to water data and information needed to support adaptation to climate change. Key next steps suggested in the report have informed the supporting actions described below and include:

- strengthen observational data systems;
- prioritize observations for understanding water supply availability;
- step up the pace of systematic reanalysis of existing observational data to bring statistics used for design and planning purposes up to date with current conditions;
- strengthen links between water observational data and climate models;
- provide water datasets to an interagency climate data portal;
- make strengthening of water data systems a priority in the National Action Plan for freshwater resources; and
- strengthen Federal agency coordination to improve data quality and accessibility.

Supporting Actions

Key actions to support this recommendation include:

3. Strengthen data for understanding climate change impacts on water resources.

The Federal government should implement a multiagency effort, led by the Department of the Interior, to build a national Water Census describing the changing availability, quality, location, and uses of water resources. This information will be organized on a watershed basis and will be readily available to water managers and the public. The Water Census will contain:

- water demand and use information (withdrawals, return flows, and consumptive use for all major water use sectors with special data collection efforts designed to track changing water use patterns relevant to public water systems, agriculture, energy, industry, and ecosystem services);

Lead Agency:
DOI

Implementation Status:
Now

- water quantity and availability information including analysis of changes in storage (groundwater) and flow (rivers);
- analysis of changes in water quality that are critical to its use (temperature, sediment, nutrients, pathogens, salinity, waterborne contaminants); and
- identification of alternative water sources that may become available through technology advances including reuse, desalination, aquifer storage and recovery.

4. Create a formal program to align "hydroclimatic" statistics with today's climate and anticipate future changes.

This work should include evaluation of data as needed to provide water resources managers and engineers engaged in infrastructure planning, management decisions, ecosystem protection, and flood hazard mitigation with the interpretative "hydrostatistics" that they need to make good decisions as hydrological conditions change over time. Hydroclimatic statistics related to floods (e.g., 100-year flood), intense rainfall (e.g., 50-year 6-hour rainfall), streamflows (e.g., 7Q10), and water temperature (e.g., mean August water temperature) are central to water infrastructure planning, ecosystem protection, and flood hazard mitigation.

> "There is no consistent formal procedure across agencies for certifying a new method or making a new product official."
>
> Decision Support Experiments and Evaluations
> Using Seasonal-to-Interannual Forecasts
> and Observational Data:
> A Focus on Water Resources;
> U.S. Climate Change Science Program, 2008

This program should include:

- systematic nationwide updates of statistical analyses;
- research to evaluate changes in hydroclimatic conditions at several temporal and spatial scales;
- updating analytical approaches to incorporate climate change;
- ensuring the continuity and stability of the long-term data collection programs on which these statistics depend; and
- consideration of a process for endorsement or certification of updated methods and data.

Lead Agency:
DOI

Implementation Status:
Now

Additional information about needs of decisionmakers for research and updated analytical information is provided in the CCAWWG's January 2011 report, Addressing Climate Change in Long-Term Water Resources Planning and Management: User Needs for Improving Tools and Information.

5. Implement an active, reliable surveillance system for tracking waterborne disease and public health threats relevant to climate change.

The surveillance system should provide for centralized coordination of public health information with water exposure pathways including surveillance of:

- endemic disease and outbreaks associated with exposure to waterborne pathogens; and
- diseases associated with waterborne contaminant exposures (chemicals and their byproducts, toxins released by algae and cyanobacteria, etc.).

Lead Agency:
CDC

Implementation Status:
Further development

Data on waterborne disease will provide a basis for developing national profiles of current and emerging diseases that are relevant to climate change, identifying climate-sensitive disease pathways, predicting factors that trigger public-health threats, and developing control and monitoring strategies that are protective of public health.

6. Provide coastal states and communities with essential information to identify areas likely to be inundated by sea level rise.

Coastal communities need reliable maps of areas likely to be inundated by rising sea levels due to climate change in order to protect water-related infrastructure facilities (e.g., sewage treatment plants, drinking water treatment facilities, and power plants) as well as to manage natural habitats and

Lead Agency:
NOAA/USACE

Implementation Status:
Further development

resources. Development of these maps will require that the Federal government provide nationally consistent information concerning coastal topography (e.g., lidar data), coastal land subsidence, and expected storm surges. Federal agencies need to develop a strategy for providing these maps and relevant guidance in specific areas on clear schedules. This action will be closely coordinated with climate adaptation plans currently under development by the National Ocean Council.

This coordinated activity should:

- increase the availability of high-resolution elevation data in coastal areas;
- provide regionally specific projections of relative sea level changes;
- provide tools for assessing storm surge risks in coordination with changing sea levels and storm frequencies and intensities;
- ensure that all maps and other geospatial information are provided in the consistent format of the National Geospatial Reference System; and
- improve access to tools for visualizing scientific and climate data.

7. **Establish an interagency effort to expedite implementation of the newly developed wetlands mapping standard.**

Wetlands play a critical role in supporting resilience of watersheds and water resources to a changing climate. As temperatures warm, some wetlands will disappear and others may be created. Understanding the changes in location, size and functions of wetlands will require accurate maps. Federal agencies are now implementing a newly developed wetland mapping standard that will facilitate efforts across Federal agencies and State, Tribal, and local governments, such as State Wildlife Action Plans. This effort, however, is underfunded and will not be completed for many years at current funding levels. This recommendation calls for an interagency effort to complete this work across the country on a significantly expedited schedule.

Lead Agency:
DOI

Implementation Status:
Now

Recommendation 3
Strengthen assessment of vulnerability of water resources to climate change

Extreme weather events, sea level rise, shifting precipitation and runoff patterns, temperature changes, and resulting changes in water quality and availability all have potentially significant implications for the operations of water sector utilities. To adapt to climate change, water resource managers must first determine the degrees of risk and vulnerability in their systems. Consistent with other approved Federal guidelines and documents, the Workgroup adopted the Intergovernmental Panel on Climate Change (IPCC) definition of vulnerability from its fourth assessment:

> Vulnerability is the degree to which a system is susceptible to, and unable to cope with, adverse effects of climate change, including climate variability and extremes. Vulnerability is a function of the character, magnitude, and rate of climate change and variation to which a system is exposed, its sensitivity, and its adaptive capacity... (IPCC, 2007b)

Risk can simply be defined as "exposure to the chance of injury or loss; a hazard or dangerous choice." (IPCC, 2007b) Risk assessment can be defined as:

> Risk assessment characterizes the nature and magnitude of risks to a physical system from stressors that may be present in the environment. It represents the determination of quantitative or qualitative value of risk related to a concrete situation and a recognized threat (also called hazard). Risk managers use this information to help them decide how to protect a system from stressors. (IPCC, 2007b)

Risk assessments can generally be conducted two different ways—using a top-down approach or using a bottom-up approach. A top-down risk assessment uses global circulation models and other globally and nationally derived data and scenarios and applies them to regions by downscaling. A bottom-up risk assessment uses regional and local knowledge, data, and information to determine the risk of an area to identified hazards.

Federal agencies have made substantial investments in the development of climate change assessment tools related to water resources. Some examples include:

- Environmental Protection Agency (EPA) work to modify existing risk assessment methodologies (e.g., natural disaster and terrorism) for drinking water and wastewater utility owners and operators to consider climate change impacts, including the Climate Resilience Evaluation and Awareness Tool (CREAT) (see Appendix F);
- The July 30, 2010 Memorandum of Understanding between the Department of Commerce and the Department of the Interior to establish a framework to enable better decisions and policies relating to understanding climate change, assessing vulnerability, and improving science, data, and technical assistance;
- National Oceanic and Atmospheric Administration's (NOAA) work to expand pilot projects for regional drought early warning information systems under the National Integrated Drought Information System (NIDIS);
- NOAA Vulnerability Assessment Techniques and Applications (VATA) for coastal communities and the joint training on vulnerability assessment of fish and wildlife and other natural resources for managers (see Appendix F); and
- US Army Corps of Engineers' (USACE) Dam Safety Action Classification tool (see Appendix F).

Existing efforts to develop vulnerability tools have focused on categories of infrastructure that may be at risk as a result of climate change or may need to change operations. These infrastructure facilities are often critical to protecting human health, life and property. More attention will need to be given in the future to vulnerability assessment tools for ecosystems and the services they provide.

Supporting Actions

The following actions support this recommendation.

8. Publish guidance on the use of modeled projections for water resource applications.

A barrier to expanded use of climate change vulnerability assessment tools is the difficulty in translating modeled projections of long-term changes in water resource conditions expected as a result of warmer temperatures into program and project plans. Although climate projections are available at large scales, in some cases there is a need to "downscale" the model outputs so that they are more relevant for hydrologic applications in specific watersheds and facilities for which assessments are being conducted. Federal agencies are in the process of developing downscaled modeled outputs, and guidance on how to use these products would help decisionmakers make better use of them. Federal agencies should also make more widely available existing plans and schedules for improvements to models and tools for projecting changes in water conditions as a result of climate change and evaluate the performance of various downscaling approaches.

Lead Agency:
NOAA

Implementation Status:
Further development

9. Develop a Federal Internet portal to provide current, relevant, and high quality information on water resources and climate change.

This portal will support public and private water resource management decisions such as climate vulnerability assessments. Currently, core water data and hydrostatistics are not readily available to water resource managers at a single Internet site. The portal should also offer data applications and tools for assessing vulnerability of water programs or facilities to climate change. A prototype portal should be developed for one group of decisionmakers and expanded upon successful development and evaluation. This effort should build on activities such as the National Integrated Drought Information System (NIDIS) (which has demonstrated the value of a single government portal focused on a challenge); the U.S. Global Change Research Program (which is currently working on an interagency global portal that could support or contribute to this action) and the USACE lead Federal Support Toolbox for Integrated Water Resources Management (which also supports and contributes to this action).

Lead Agency:
NOAA/USACE

Implementation Status:
Further development

Contributions to this portal should be made using nationally and internationally agreed to data standards and mechanisms. One such example is the Group on Earth Observations (GEO) which has implemented and tested standards for interchange and interoperability using Open Geospatial Consortium compliant Web services and netCDF data protocols. The portal should also leverage advances and lessons learned in the Consortium of Universities for the Advancement of Hydrologic Science, Inc (CUAHSI) Hydrologic Information System (HIS) and CalAdapt, a tool developed in California by a collaboration of the private and public sectors and universities for exchanging and visualizing data and information related to climate adaptation.

10. Develop a pilot climate change vulnerability index for a major category of water facilities and use pilot findings to support vulnerability assessments by other facility categories.

An index of vulnerability should be developed for a major category of water facilities (e.g., sewage treatment facilities, water supply infrastructure, or flood control dams) to demonstrate an approach to assessing the relative risk of climate change impacts to facilities. Such an assessment could focus on vulnerabilities in particular geographic regions, such as vulnerability to drought in the west or floods in the northeast. The results of an index assessment can be used to set priorities for implementation of climate adaptation responses.

Lead Agency:
NOAA/DOI

Implementation Status:
Further development

This pilot index for a single category of facility should serve as a proof of concept for developing vulnerability indices to support assessments by a range of other water facilities and sectors. This work should be conducted in coordination with complementary vulnerability assessment activities to support the water sector, such as those identified in the MOU between DOI and DOC/NOAA, and the efforts of EPA's Climate Ready Water Utilities program. Over the long term, this could support development of a database of vulnerable infrastructure to support prioritization for infrastructure investments.

11. Continue development of tools and approaches that build capacity for water-related institutions to conduct vulnerability assessments and implement appropriate responses.

There are several important efforts now underway to support vulnerability assessments. For example, EPA has successfully developed the Climate Ready Estuaries Program and is in the process of developing a Climate Ready Water Utilities program. Both programs provide climate assessment tools tailored to the needs of a particular water institution or program and have the potential to promote effective climate impact assessments and to establish public recognition of climate adaptation efforts. In addition, the USBR report addressing climate change issues in western basins provides useful information for assessing climate vulnerability, such as downscaled impacts information. Existing programs of this type should be expanded and similar approaches should be adapted and applied by other Federal agencies, irrigation districts, power plants, ports, and dams and reservoirs as appropriate. Vulnerability assessments can also be used to identify those aquatic species and habitats most likely to be in need of conservation actions as a result of climate change.

Lead Agency:
EPA

Implementation Status:
Now

12. Assess vulnerability of watersheds and aquatic systems in National Forests and Grasslands.

The U.S. Department of Agriculture's (USDA) Forest Service is implementing assessments of the condition of forested watersheds in each of the agency regions. These condition assessments will be expanded into assessments of the vulnerability of watersheds and aquatic systems to climate and nonclimate stresses in multiple future scenarios. The watershed vulnerability assessments will be integrated with assessments of the vulnerability of terrestrial resources and of social and economic attributes and used to guide adaptation strategies in forest planning.

Lead Agency:
USDA Forest Service

Implementation Status:
Now

13. Promote free and open access to authoritative climate change science and water resources data.

Data and information should be available to decisionmakers, researchers, and the public freely and openly and in formats that readily fit the needs of users. Current law (15 U.S.C. §1534) mandates cost recovery for access to certain science data for most users outside of the Federal and State governments. To enhance the use of authoritative Federal climate science information and data for all decisionmakers, Congress should be encouraged to eliminate mandatory cost recovery for this information. This recommendation would likely require changing the fee access structure in current law.

Lead Agency:
NOAA

Implementation Status:
Further development

Recommendation 4
Expand water use efficiency

Water resources in the United States, already under stress because of growing population, contamination, demand to meet ecosystem needs, and drought, will be further challenged by climate change. Making more efficient use of water can extend the availability of current supplies, reduce competition among sectors, save energy, reduce the cost of water system operations through reduced water use, protect the environment, and prepare for increased climate-driven variability in the hydrologic cycle.

Water use efficiency has several aspects that encompass:

- Efficiency — using as little water as needed to do the job, or
- Conservation — using less water,

- Productivity—getting more output per unit of water, and
- Substitution—using alternative sources as a means to match the quality of water with the intended use.

There are currently a number of programs across the Federal agencies that have a focus on water use efficiency. Types of programs include research and development, regulatory/policy development, technical assistance/training, funding, voluntary/incentive programs, and public education/outreach. However, there are several significant Federal efforts underway—some of which are just beginning—that deserve special attention and continued support. These include the DOI WaterSMART initiative, the U.S. Geological Survey (USGS) Water Census, EPA's WaterSense program, the USDA Natural Resources Conservation Service's (NRCS) Agricultural Water Enhancement Program, DOE research development and demonstration (RD&D) on water-efficient clean energy practices, and a Federally requested assessment by the National Academy of Sciences of water reuse as an alternative water supply. There are also activities to advance water use efficiency being carried out by other entities, including States, local governments and affiliated agencies, green building programs, and nongovernmental organizations.

The Workgroup considered the following barriers as it developed recommendations:

Information End-users do not have sufficient information on their water use to compare their usage rates to those of others and to recognize the benefits of improved water use efficiency.

Pricing and incentives Because water is often undervalued and underpriced, there is little incentive to use water more efficiently.

Coordination Improved coordination on water use management issues across Federal agencies and within agencies is needed to improve efficiency gains.

Planning There is inadequate consideration of water use efficiency when making decisions on water supply management, land use, and energy development.

Education There is a general lack of public awareness and education on the benefits of water and how to use it more efficiently.

Development and adoption of water-efficient technology and practices There is inadequate effort to advance research, development, and adoption of cost-effective technology and approaches that could improve water use efficiency or facilitate use of alternative sources.

Although the Federal government has a direct role in making water management decisions where it controls water resources, its role is largely limited to serving as a source of information, providing guidance, conducting research and development, and supplying funding to provide incentives for actions. The recommendations that follow reflect that general role for the U.S. government.

Supporting Actions

The following actions support this recommendation.

14. **Develop nationally consistent metrics for water use efficiency in key sectors and report water efficiency information in nationally consistent formats.**

To be able to make sound decisions on improving efficiency, and to ensure transparency and program accountability, it is important to understand how water is used. The USGS has published national-scale summaries of water use every 5 years since 1950 and the Energy Information Agency (EIA) collects data annually on water withdrawals, consumption, discharge, and water sources directly from power plants. The most recent USGS report indicates that thermoelectric power, irrigation, and public supply were the largest water users by volume—making up 91 percent of the total water diverted for use in the country. Improvements in water use efficiency will require implementation of actions that reduce both water withdrawal and consumptive water use (water withdrawn from a source for any use and not returned to that source).

A common adage is: "You can't manage what you don't measure." Although publicly supplied water is metered in more locations than is irrigation water, there are still significant improvements that can be made in all sectors to understand use. Furthermore, nationally consistent metrics for key sectors expressing water withdrawal and use on a per capita, per acre, or per kilowatt basis should be developed. These

Lead Agency:
EPA/USDA/DOE

Implementation Status:
Now

metrics would provide decision makers and the public with information on relative water efficiency and the potential for water efficiency improvements that would have both cost savings and environmental benefits. It is important that this type of effort be undertaken in cooperation with States, producers, landowners, and others and that it be based on voluntary incentives rather than mandatory reporting.

15. **Consider making water use efficiency an explicit consideration in the revision of Principles and Standards for water resources projects and in the new NEPA guidance on climate change.**

The Council on Environmental Quality is working with other Federal agencies to review and revise the 1983 "Economic and Environmental Principles and Guidelines for Water and Related Land Resources Implementation Studies." This effort is intended to ensure that Federal water resources planning, including analysis of major water infrastructure projects, will both improve the economic well-being of the Nation and protect and restore the environment. The proposed revised "Principles and Requirements" have been published for public review and comment and additional comments were received from the National Academy of Sciences in December 2010. A final,

Lead Agency:
CEQ

Implementation Status:
Now

revised "Principles and Requirements" document is expected to be approved in late-2011. As improvements are made to the Principles and Requirements, options for improving water use efficiency should be an explicit consideration.

In a related effort, CEQ has proposed guidance for improved implementation of the National Environmental Policy Act (NEPA). On February 18, 2010, CEQ proposed guidance for consideration of the effects of climate change and greenhouse gas emissions. Although the draft guidance does not specifically address water projects, many major water resources projects, or projects that rely on water (e.g., energy facilities) would be covered by the approaches described in the draft guidance. The draft guidance speaks to consideration of greenhouse gas impacts of projects, including analysis of alternatives to mitigate climate impacts. The draft guidance also describes how climate changes should be addressed in identifying "reasonably foreseeable future conditions" (for example, declining water supplies) and comparing the incremental differences in water demand required by alternatives. In addition, opportunities for agencies to recognize the potential for water use efficiency, which, in turn, results in energy conservation and resulting greenhouse gas reductions should be considered as the draft guidance is finalized. The final guidance on considering Greenhouse Gas Emissions and Climate Change in the NEPA process is expected to be approved by the end of 2011.

16. Enhance coordination among Federal water efficiency programs and improve program effectiveness, including creating a "toolbox" of key practices.

Several existing Federal programs now make important contributions to water use efficiency. These programs should be maintained and, where possible, expanded. However, because the programs currently operate independently, they may be missing opportunities to share best practices and approaches, particularly in specific geographic areas that are under water-stressed conditions. The DOI WaterSMART Clearinghouse is an example of a valuable mechanism that will facilitate information sharing for programs, government grants, and funding related to water conservation.

Additionally, agencies should enhance coordination and information exchange with Federal research, development, and demonstration (RD&D) planning efforts to highlight key technology and data gaps and identify priority RD&D needs. Agencies also should establish a formal coordination mechanism and a cross-agency "toolbox" that includes key practices, such as pricing signals. In addition, the Federal government should promote institutional commitment to water conservation and reuse by making annual awards for proven efforts and calling out innovative practices or approaches that have the potential to result in significant water conservation or reuse if adopted widely.

> **Lead Agency:**
> DOI/EPA/DOE/USACE
> **Implementation Status:**
> Now

Finally, Federal agencies are now working to implement the environmental sustainability goals established in Executive Order 13514, including the goal of a 26-percent improvement in water efficiency by 2020. Progress toward the environmental goals is reported on agency "scorecards" and innovative approaches that are proven to be effective by Federal agencies should be recognized and communicated to State, Tribal, and local governments and the private sector.

Recommendation 5
Support integrated water resources management

The Intergovernmental Panel on Climate Change (IPCC) states that integrated water resources management (IWRM) should be the "instrument to explore adaptation measures to climate change." According to the Global Water Partnership, IWRM "promotes the coordinated development and management of water, land, and related resources, in order to maximize the resultant economic and social welfare in an equitable manner without compromising the sustainability of vital ecosystems."

Climate change will increase the stress on water resources and this will require more collaboration among Federal agencies and Federal, State, Tribal and, local governments, stakeholders, and countries with which the United States shares transboundary waters. Climate change is just one of the stressors affecting water resources. Changes in water demand and alterations in the watershed are also key stressors. Managing the risks from a changing climate cannot occur in isolation from other major stressors and effective water resources management requires integration of response to all stressors and a commitment to adaptive management.

Planning is always conducted under conditions of uncertainty. Water agencies should seek solutions

> "…there will have to be a 'paradigm shift' from the deterministic view embodied in the 'Principles and Guidelines' (WRC; 1973, 1983), based on a view of relatively stationary climate, to a much more flexible set of multi-objective evaluation principles and procedures that more appropriately account for the full range of social, environmental, and regional economic dimensions of water infrastructure under a wide range of uncertain climate scenarios."
>
> Eugene Stakhiv; Workshop on Nonstationarity, Hydrologic Frequency Analysis, and Water Management Proceedings, 2010.

that encompass a range of potential future conditions. Adaptive management may be the most effective way of dealing with future climate impacts. Adaptive management requires sustained, coordinated monitoring and ongoing analysis of data in order to incorporate the most effective structural and operational adjustments in response to observed system changes. Adaptive management also requires institutions and funding to reevaluate project and program performance and to revise decisions on the basis of the most recent information.

Supporting Actions

Actions to support integrated water resources management are described below.

17. Work with States and interstate bodies (e.g., river basin commissions) to provide assistance needed to incorporate IWRM into their planning and programs, paying particular attention to climate change adaptation issues.

The Water Resources Planning Act of 1965 authorizes river basin water commissions to provide for coordination of water resources management on a large watershed scale. The establishment of river basin management authorities or commissions is considered one of the essential components of a successful IWRM strategy.

> "To foster IWRM, an appropriate role for the Federal government may be that of integrator. Many participants in this initiative extolled the supporting role of the interstate organizations as vanguards in furthering integrated approaches and outcomes. The fragmentation of governance mechanisms at all government levels hinders government ability to support state's water resources planning…"
>
> National Report: Responding to National Water Resources Challenges, US Army Corps of Engineers, 2010

In their 2006 report on "Interstate Water Solutions for the New Millennium," the Interstate Council on Water Policy (ICWP) noted "a strong state/federal partnership is necessary to enhance the efficiency and capacity of integrated water resource management efforts."

As an initial first step in expanding or strengthening river basin governance, Federal agencies should work with States, interstate commissions, and river basin commissions to provide the financial and technical assistance needed to establish or strengthen their ability to conduct a range of water resources planning functions. Priority should be given

Lead Agency:
USACE

Implementation Status:
Further development

to proposals to address climate change adaptation challenges such as coordinated management of water supply and energy production, planning for limited water availability, integrating the management of groundwater and surface water supplies, and coordination to protect the health of large aquatic ecosystems stressed by climate change, including downstream coastal areas.

18. Revise Federal water project planning standards to address climate change.

Planning "principles" articulated in the draft revised "Principles and Requirements" document (described above in supporting action 15) include new emphasis on addressing risk and uncertainty, including the consequences of climate change on future water resources projects and programs. The final, revised "Principles and Requirements" document is expected to be approved in late 2011. Federal agencies should continue this effort and give priority to maintaining recognition of the importance of

Lead Agency:
CEQ

Implementation Status:
Now

accounting for future climate change in Federal water resources planning and applying adaptive management principles to this work.

19. **Working with States, review flood risk management planning and drought management planning to identify "best practices" to prepare for hydrologic extremes in a changing climate.**

With the potential for more extreme hydrologic conditions as a result of climate change, effective planning for the management of flood and drought risk is a strategic national concern because of the potential for cascading economic and public safety impacts where adequate planning has not occurred.

Flood and drought management and preparedness are the leading edge of a practical adaptation strategy as part of IWRM. Flood and drought management have often been characterized by reactive response activities after a flood or while a drought is occurring. More efforts and resources should be directed at proactive preparedness to reduce vulnerability to floods and droughts. This work needs to recognize that the frequency and magnitude of future floods and droughts is likely to increase and that the historical record is no longer a reliable predictor of future conditions.

Lead Agency:
USACE

Implementation Status:
Further development

In addition, State, Tribal, and local governments play an important role in flood and drought preparedness and mitigation. Land use decisions, which are a determinant of vulnerability, are primarily a function of these governments. Federal programs need to be better integrated with State, Tribal, and local programs and Federal investment should shift from crisis response toward an integrated and proactive risk management strategy. In some States, "Silver Jacket" interagency teams provide well-trained and proactive Federal-State-local efforts at the State and local scale to coordinate a comprehensive flood risk management program (for more information, see http://www.fema.gov/mitigationbp/file/3505_silver_jackets.pdf).

As a first step in strengthening coordination among Federal, State, Tribal, and local agencies on drought and flood issues, Federal agencies should work closely with States to review flood and drought planning activities. Key goals of this effort should be to identify "best practices" that can be shared with others, including the degree of coordination between flood and drought management, cooperative efforts with Federal agencies (e.g., Silver Jackets), the extent to which new information concerning hydrologic variations is reflected in plans, and innovative or especially useful planning or coordination mechanisms. The development of the National Integrated Drought Information System (NIDIS) by multiple Federal agencies, with NOAA as the lead agency, is a good example of a cooperative project to address information needs in this area.

20. **Develop benchmarks for incorporating adaptive management into water project designs, operational procedures, and planning strategies.**

A planning strategy for climate change is to promote mid-course corrections in response to new information. As noted above, adaptive management is a key element of IWRM. According to the National Research Council, "Adaptive management promotes flexible decisionmaking that can be adjusted in the face of uncertainties as outcomes from management actions and other events become better understood" (National Research Council, 2004). Federal agencies should develop benchmarks for incorporating adaptive management into their planning and operations and should allocate a portion of project funds for monitoring for adaptive management.

Lead Agency:
USACE

Implementation Status:
Now

Recommendation 6
Support training and outreach to build response capability

In communities across America, solutions to climate-driven water challenges will often come from local experts equipped with the right mix of local knowledge, technical expertise, resources and tools, and understanding of climate change impacts and adaptation measures. Today, the workforce that manages water resources programs at all levels of government and in the private sector is generally not well prepared to recognize the implications of a changing climate or to make complex risk management decisions that address climate change.

Capacity building and education are inextricably connected. Human capacity in the context of climate adaptation—the ability to understand, adapt, and innovate in the face of a changing climate—will be built through educational and developmental activities at all levels, from traditional education to professional development, outreach, and informal learning.

The current water and science education paradigm does not prepare citizens (students, workforce, others) to understand, interpret, and address the water challenges posed by a changing climate. Until now, instruction has commonly been based on a model that assumes that information leads to knowledge and knowledge leads to engagement—including types of action that will be needed to adapt to a changing climate. Unfortunately, the vast majority of citizens, employees, and decision-makers have limited engagement in addressing water issues.

To help water managers and others understand and appreciate the value of water as a shared resource that is increasingly stressed in a changing climate, a new paradigm for climate-water education is needed that values cross-disciplinary education, instruction and training. Programs should focus on holistic solutions (i.e., crosscutting solutions for agriculture, energy, environment, and communities) for water resource management in response to a changing climate. Education must come from a host of sources and through a variety of mechanisms including traditional, nontraditional, and informal learning. In addition, programs must be tailored to audience needs as reflected by age, geography, and varying cultural backgrounds.

Supporting Actions

The following specific actions are proposed to support this recommendation.

21. **Establish a core training program related to climate change science for local, Tribal, State, and Federal water resources managers.**

    Federal, State, Tribal, and local water resources managers need basic information and guidance on a range of issues associated with climate-related data, models, analytic approaches, and local and regional interpretation of climate change impacts and adaptation options.

    Federal agencies should collaborate to develop and provide a core, cross-disciplinary training program that would provide State, Tribal, and local managers (as well as other natural resource, land, and wildlife managers) with a solid foundation in climate change information and issues. Training should be conducted in different regions of the country and

    > **Lead Agency:**
    > USBR/USACE/NOAA
    >
    > **Implementation Status:**
    > Now

    provide easy access to Web-based curriculum, perhaps in cooperation with "continuing education" requirements of various professional groups, such as water and wastewater treatment operators. This work should be coordinated with planning for a Climate Change Learning Center by the U.S. Fish and Wildlife Service.

In addition to key information concerning climate change and its impacts on water resources, a training program can also share information concerning promising approaches and practices to facilitate water resources adaptation to a changing climate. For example, a training program might provide information on water efficiency tools and techniques and share practices that support watershed resilience through enhanced groundwater recharge and better management of stormwater, such as "green infrastructure" and "low impact development".

22. Focus existing youth outreach programs on climate change and water issues.

Federal agencies should make climate change and water resources a key element of existing youth outreach programs, such as the USDA 4H program and the nonprofit Project WET (Water Education for Teachers), and expand Federal agency environmental education programs to target climate and water resources.

> **Lead Agency:**
> USDA
>
> **Implementation Status:**
> Now

23. Engage Water Resources Research Institutes at land grant colleges and Tribal colleges in applied climate change adaptation research and capacity building through annual climate change grant awards.

Investing in existing Water Resources Research Institutes has the double benefit of generating relevant research in states throughout the country and of engaging graduate students in issues related to climate change and water. Graduate students with research experience in these areas will then be available to move into positions with water resource management agencies at the Federal, State, Tribal, and local level. This work should be done in partnership with local institutions and utilities.

> **Lead Agency:**
> DOI
>
> **Implementation Status:**
> Further development

24. Increase graduate level fellowships in water management and climate change.

Support fellowships for graduate students with an interest in climate change and water research or management issues that include an avenue to Federal employment. Federal agencies could look to trained graduate students as a recruitment mechanism to meet long term staffing needs related to water resources research and management. The existing John A. Knauss Fellowships in Marine Policy should be considered as a model.

> **Lead Agency:**
> NOAA
>
> **Implementation Status:**
> Further development

Conclusion

A changing climate will have important consequences for the Nation's freshwater resources. Today, the community of water resource managers is increasingly informed about climate impacts and engaged in defining response actions. Federal agencies with water resources management responsibility have become increasingly engaged in understanding climate impacts and developing response actions. This National Action Plan is an initial effort to provide a common foundation of useful information and to describe priority response actions for Federal agencies. Information on climate impacts on freshwater resources will improve in the coming years. And understanding of the contributions of various response actions described in this Plan will contribute to improved and more effective response actions. More important, however, for the long term success of this effort is for the broader community of water resources managers to continue to engage and address the challenges of a changing climate.

Hoover Dam

Selected References

Asrar, G., J.A. Kaye, and P. Morel. (2001). NASA Research Strategy for Earth System Science: Climate Component. Bulletin of the American Meteorological Society, 82, 1309-1329. Retrieved from http://www-nacip.ucsd.edu/BAMS8270701AsrarKayeMorel.pdf.

Barker, T., I. Bashmakov, A. Alharthi, M. Amann, L. Cifuentes, J. Drexhage, M. Duan, O. Edenhofer, B. Flannery, M. Grubb, M. Hoogwijk, F. I. Ibitoye, C. J. Jepma, W. A. Pizer, and K. Yamaji. (2007). Mitigation from a Cross-sectoral Perspective. In Climate Change 2007: Mitigation. Contribution of Working Group III to the Fourth Assessment Report of the Intergovernmental Panel on Climate Change. [Metz, B., O. Davidson, P. Bosch, R. Dave, and L. Meyer (eds.)]. New York: Cambridge University Press. Retrieved from http://www.ipcc.ch/pdf/assessment-report/ar4/wg3/ar4-wg3-chapter11.pdf.

Barsugli, J., C. Anderson, J.B. Smith, and J.M. Vogel. (2009). Options for Improving Climate Modeling to Assist Water Utility Planning for Climate Change. Water Utility Climate Alliance. Retrieved from http://www.wucaonline.org/assets/pdf/actions_whitepaper_120909.pdf.

Bates, B.C., Z.W. Kundzewicz, S. Wu, and J.P. Palutikof (Editors). (2008). Climate Change and Water. (Intergovernmental Panel on Climate Change Technical Paper VI). Geneva: IPCC Secretariat, Working Group II, Technical Support Unit. Retrieved from http://www.ipcc.ch/pdf/technical-papers/climate-change-water-en.pdf.

Beller-Simms, N., H. Ingram, D. Feldman, N. Mantua, K.L. Jacobs, and A. Waple. (2008). Decision-Support Experiments and Evaluations Using Seasonal to Interannual Forecasts and Observational Data: A Focus on Water resources (Synthesis and Assessment Product 5.3). Washington, DC: U.S. Global Change Research Program and Climate Change Research Initiative, U.S. Climate Change Science Program Office. Retrieved from http://www.climatescience.gov/Library/sap/sap5-3/final-report/sap5-3-final-all.pdf.

Bierbaum, R.M., D. Brown, and J. McAlpine. (2008). Coping with Climate Change: National Summit Proceedings. Ann Arbor, MI: University of Michigan Press.

Bindoff, N.L., J. Willebrand, V. Artale, A, Cazenave, J.M. Gregory, S. Gulev, K. Hanawa, C. Le Quéré, S. Levitus, Y. Nojiri, C.K. Shum, L.D. Talley, and A.S. Unnikrishnan. (2007). Observations: Oceanic Climate Change and Sea Level. In Climate Change 2007: The Physical Science Basis. Contribution of Working Group I to the Fourth Assessment Report of the Intergovernmental Panel on Climate Change. [Solomon, S., D. Qin, M. Manning, Z. Chen, M. Marquis, K.B. Averyt, M. Tignor, and H.L. Miller (eds.)]. New York: Cambridge University Press. Retrieved from http://www.ipcc.ch/pdf/assessment-report/ar4/wg1/ar4-wg1-chapter5.pdf.

Brown, Casey. (2010). The End of Reliability. Journal of Water Resources Planning and Management. March/April 2010. P. 143-145. http://scitation.aip.org/getpdf/servlet/GetPDFServlet?filetype=pdf&id=JWRMD5000136000002000143000001&idtype=cvips&doi=10.1061/(ASCE)WR.1943-5452.65&prog=normal&bypassSSO=1.

Burkett, V., J.O. Codignotto, D.L. Forbes, N. Mimura, R.J. Beamish, and V. Ittekkot. (2001). Coastal Zones and Marine Ecosystems. In Climate Change 2001: Impacts, Adaptation and Vulnerability. Contribution of Working Group II to the Third Assessment Report of the Intergovernmental Panel on Climate Change. [McCarthy, J.J., O.F. Canziani, N.A. Leary, D.J. Dokken, and K.S. White (eds.)]. New York: Cambridge University Press. Retrieved from http://www.grida.no/climate/ipcc_tar/wg2/index.htm.

CalAdapt. California Natural Resources Agency, accessed July 18, 2011. Available at: http://cal-adapt.org/.

California Department of Water Resources. (2005). California Water Plan Update 2005: A Framework for Action (Department of Water Resources Bulletin 160-05). Sacramento, CA: Division of Planning and Local Assistance, California Department of Water Resources. Retrieved from http://www.waterplan.water.ca.gov/previous/cwpu2005/index.cfm.

Christensen, J.H., B. Hewitson, A. Busuioc, A. Chen, X. Gao, I. Held, R. Jones, R.K. Kolli, W.-T. Kwon, R. Laprise, V. Magaña Rueda, L. Mearns, C.G. Menéndez, J. Räisänen, A. Rinke, A. Sarr, and P. Whetton. (2007). Regional Climate Projections. In Climate Change 2007: The Physical Science Basis. Contribution of Working Group I to the Fourth Assessment Report of the Intergovernmental Panel on Climate Change. [Solomon, S., D. Qin, M. Manning, Z. Chen, M. Marquis, K.B. Averyt, M. Tignor, and H.L. Miller (eds.)]. New York: Cambridge University Press. Retrieved from http://www.ipcc.ch/pdf/assessment-report/ar4/wg1/ar4-wg1-chapter11.pdf.

Clean Water America Alliance (CWAA). (2009). A Call to Action: The Need for an Integrated National Water Policy (National Dialogue Report). Washington, DC: Clean Water America Alliance. Retrieved from http://www.cleanwateramericaalliance.org/pdfs/2009-11-16report.pdf.

Cohen, S., K. Miller, K. Duncan, E. Gregorich, P. Groffman, P. Kovacs, V. Magaña, D. McKnight, E. Mills, and D. Schimel. (2001). Climate Change 2001: Impacts, Adaptation, and Vulnerability. Contribution of Working Group II to the Third Assessment Report of the Intergovernmental Panel on Climate Change. [McCarthy, J.J., O.F. Canziani, N.A. Leary, D.J. Dokken, K.S. White (eds.)]. New York: Cambridge University Press. Retrieved from http://www.grida.no/climate/ipcc_tar/wg2/548.htm.

Consortium for Energy Efficiency (CEE). (2007). Initiative Description: CEE National Municipal Water and Wastewater Facility Initiative. Retrieved from http://www.cee1.org/ind/mot-sys/ww/ww-init-des.pdf.

Denman, K.L., G. Brasseur, A. Chidthaisong, P. Ciais, P. M. Cox, R. E. Dickinson, D. Hauglustaine, C. Heinze, E. Holland, D. Jacob, U. Lohmann, S. Ramachandran, P. Leite da Silva Dias, S. C. Wofsy, and X. Zhang. (2007). Couplings between Changes in the Climate System and Biogeochemistry. In Climate Change 2007: The Physical Science Basis. Contribution of Working Group I to the Fourth Assessment Report of the Intergovernmental Panel on Climate Change [Solomon, S., D. Qin, M. Manning, Z. Chen, M. Marquis, K.B. Averyt, M. Tignor, and H.L. Miller (eds.)]. New York: Cambridge University Press. Retrieved from http://www.ipcc.ch/pdf/assessment-report/ar4/wg1/ar4-wg1-chapter7.pdf.

Dooley, J.J., R.T. Dahowski, C.L. Davidson, M.A. Wise, N. Gupta, S.H. Kim, and E.L. Malone. (2006). Carbon Dioxide Capture and Geologic Storage: A Core Element of a Global Energy Technology Strategy to Address Climate Change (Technology Report from the Second Phase of the Global Energy Technology Strategy Program PNNL-15296). College Park, MD: Battelle, Joint Global Change Research Institute, Pacific Northwest National Laboratory. Retrieved from http://www.pnl.gov/gtsp/docs/ccs_report.pdf.

Electric Power Research Institute (EPRI). (2002). Water and Sustainability (Volume 3): U.S. Water Consumption for Power Production--The Next Half Century (Report Number 1006786). Palo Alto, CA: Electric Power Research Institute. Retrieved from http://www.epri.com. (This report is downloadable from the EPRI Web site.)

Energy Information Administration (EIA). (2004). Table 1.1. Net Generation by Energy Source: Total (All Sectors), 1990 through January 2004. Washington, DC: Energy Information Administration. Retrieved from http://www.eia.doe.gov//cneaf/electricity/epm/table1_1.html.

Environmental Protection Agency (EPA). (1986). Ambient Aquatic Life Water Quality Criteria for Pentachlorophenol (EPA-440-5-86-009). Washington, DC: U.S. Environmental Protection Agency, Office of Water. Retrieved from http://www.epa.gov/waterscience/criteria/1980docs.htm.

—. (1999). 1999 Update of Ambient Water Quality Criteria for Ammonia (EPA-822-R-99-014). Washington, DC: U.S. Environmental Protection Agency, Office of Water. Retrieved from http://www.epa.gov/waterscience/criteria/ammonia/99update.pdf.

—. (2002). Clean Water and Drinking Water Infrastructure Gap Analysis (EPA-816-R-02-020). Washington, DC: U.S. Environmental Protection Agency, Office of Water. Retrieved from http://www.epa.gov/waterinfrastructure/infrastructuregap.html.

—. (2005). Greenhouse Gas Mitigation Potential in U.S. Forestry and Agriculture (EPA 430-R-05-006). Washington, DC: U.S. Environmental Protection Agency, Office of Atmospheric Programs. Retrieved from http://www.epa.gov/sequestration/pdf/greenhousegas2005.pdf.

—. (2006). Wastewater Management Fact Sheet: Energy Conservation. Washington, DC: U.S. Environmental Protection Agency, Office of Water.

—. 2007a). Climate Change—Science. Retrieved from http://www.epa.gov/climatechange/science/index.html.

—. 2007b). Climate Change–Science: Temperature Changes. Retrieved from http://www.epa.gov/climatechange/science/recenttc.html.

—. 2007c). Climate Change–Science: Future Temperature Changes. Retrieved from http://www.epa.gov/climatechange/science/futuretc.html.

—. 2007d). Climate Change–Science: Precipitation and Storm Changes. Retrieved from http://www.epa.gov/climatechange/science/recentpsc.html.

—. 2007e). Climate Change–Science: Future Precipitation and Storm Changes. Retrieved from http://www.epa.gov/climatechange/science/futurepsc.html.

—. 2007f). Climate Change–Science: Sea Level Changes. Retrieved from http://www.epa.gov/climatechange/science/recentslc.html.

—. (2007g). Climate Change–Science: Future Sea Level Changes. Retrieved from http://www.epa.gov/climatechange/science/futureslc.html.

—. (2007h). Climate Change–Health and Environmental Effects: Water Quality. Retrieved from http://www.epa.gov/climatechange/effects/water/quality.html.

—. (2007i). Climate Change–Health and Environmental Effects: Water Availability. Retrieved from http://www.epa.gov/climatechange/effects/water/availability.html.

—. (2007j). Climate Change–Health and Environmental Effects: Water Resources in North America. Retrieved from http://www.epa.gov/climatechange/effects/usregions.html.

—. (2007k). Climate Change–Health and Environmental Effects: Coral Reefs. Retrieved from http://www.epa.gov/climatechange/effects/eco_coral.html, accessed on February 8, 2008.

—. (2007l). Climate Change–Health and Environmental Effects: Coastal Zones and Sea Level Rise. Retrieved from http://www.epa.gov/climatechange/effects/coastal/index.html.

—. (2007m). Inventory of U.S. Greenhouse Gas Emissions and Sinks: 1990-2005 (EPA 430-R-07-002). Washington, DC: U.S. Environmental Protection Agency. Retrieved from http://www.epa.gov/climatechange/emissions/usinventoryreport.html.

—. (2007n). Opportunities for and Benefits of Combined Heat and Power at Wastewater Treatment Facilities. Washington, DC: U.S. Environmental Protection Agency, Combined Heat and Power Partnership. Retrieved from http://www.epa.gov/chp/documents/wwtf_opportunities.pdf.

—. (2008). National Water Program Strategy: Response to Climate Change (EPA 800-R-08-001). Retrieved from http://water.epa.gov/scitech/climatechange/strategy.cfm.

—. (2009). Endangerment and Cause or Contribute Findings for Greenhouse Gases under Section 202(a) of the Clean Air Act, Federal Register Docket ID No. EPA-HQ-OAR-2009-0171. December 15, 2009. Retrieved from http://www.epa.gov/climatechange/endangerment.html#findings.

—. (2010a). National Water Program Strategy: Response to Climate Change–Key Action Update for 2010–2011. Retrieved from http://water.epa.gov/scitech/climatechange/.

—. (2010b). WaterSense. Retrieved from http://www.epa.gov/watersense/.

—. (2010c). Climate Ready Estuaries. Retrieved from http://www.epa.gov/cre/.

—. (2010d). Climate Ready Water Utilities. Retrieved from http://water.epa.gov/infrastructure/watersecurity/climate/index.cfm.

—. (2010e). Climate Change Vulnerability Assessments: A Review of Water Utility Practices (EPA 800-R-10-001. 832-F-06-024). Environmental Protection Agency Office of Water. Retrieved from http://water.epa.gov/scitech/climatechange/upload/Climate-Change-Vulnerability-Assessments-Sept-2010.pdf.

—. (2011). Climate Change Vulnerability Assessments: Four Case Studies of Water Utility Practices. (EPA/600/R-10/077F). Environmental Protection Agency Office of Research and Development. Retrieved from ttp://cfpub.epa.gov/ncea/global/recordisplay. cfm?deid=233808.

Field, C.B., L.D. Mortsch, M. Brklacich, D.L. Forbes, P. Kovacs, J.A. Patz, S.W. Running, and M.J. Scott. (2007). North America. In Climate Change 2007: Impacts, Adaptation and Vulnerability. Contribution of Working Group II to the Fourth Assessment Report of the Intergovernmental Panel on Climate Change. [M.L. Parry, O.F. Canziani, J.P. Palutikof, P.J. van der Linden, and C.E. Hanson, (eds.)]. New York: Cambridge University Press. Retrieved from http://www.ipcc.ch/pdf/assessment-report/ar4/wg2/ar4-wg2-chapter14.pdf.

Government Accountability Office (GAO). (2009). Climate Change Adaptation: Strategic Federal Planning Could Help Government Officials Make More Informed Decisions. Report to the Chairman, Select Committee on Energy Independence and Global Warming, House of Representatives. U.S. Government Accountability Office, October 2009 (GAO-10-113). Retrieved from http://www.gao.gov/new.items/d10113.pdf.

—. (2004). Alaska Native Villages: Villages Affected by Flooding and Erosion Have Difficulty Qualifying for Federal Assistance (GAO-04-895T). Washington, DC: GAO. Retrieved from http://www.gao.gov/cgi-bin/getrpt?GAO-04-895T.

Grumbles, B.H. (2007). Drops to Watts: Leveraging the Water and Energy Connection. Water Efficiency: The Journal for Water Conservation Professionals, July/August. Retrieved from http://www.waterefficiency.net/we_0707_guesteditora.html.

Intergovernmental Panel on Climate Change (IPCC). (2005). IPCC Special Report on Carbon Dioxide Capture and Storage. Prepared by Working Group III of the Intergovernmental Panel on Climate Change. [Metz, B., O. Davidson, H. de Coninck, M. Loos, and L. Meyer (eds.)]. New York: Cambridge University Press. Retrieved from http://www.ipcc.ch/activity/srccs/index.htm.

—. (2007a). Climate Change 2007: The Physical Science Basis. Contribution of Working Group I to the Fourth Assessment Report of the Intergovernmental Panel on Climate Change. [Solomon, S., D. Qin, M. Manning, Z. Chen, M. Marquis, K.B. Averyt, M. Tignor, and H.L. Miller (eds.)]. New York: Cambridge University Press, Cambridge. Retrieved from http://www.ipcc.ch/ipccreports/ar4-wg1.htm.

—. (2007b). Climate Change 2007: Impacts, Adaptation and Vulnerability. Contribution of Working Group II to the Fourth Assessment Report of the Intergovernmental Panel on Climate Change. [Parry, M., O. Canziani, J. Palutikof, P. van der Linden, and C. Hanson (eds.)] New York: Cambridge University Press. Retrieved from http://www.ipcc-wg2.org/.

—. (2007c). Climate Change 2007: Mitigation. Contribution of Working Group III to the Fourth Assessment Report of the Intergovernmental Panel on Climate Change. [Metz, B., O. Davidson, P. Bosch, R. Dave, and L. Meyer (eds.)]. New York: Cambridge University Press. Retrieved from http://www.mnp.nl/ipcc/pages_media/AR4-chapters.html.

—. (2008). Climate Change and Water: Technical Paper VI. [Bates, B.C., Z.W. Kundzewicz, S. Wu, and J.P. Palutikof, eds.] Geneva: IPCC Secretariat. Retrieved from http://www.ipcc.ch/publications_and_data/publications_and_data_technical_papers.shtml.

Interstate Council on Water Policy. (2006). Interstate Water Solutions for the New Millenium. Retrieved from http://www.icwp.org/cms/ic/InterstateWtrSolutionsForNewMilleniumFINAL.pdf.

Jackson, M.P., M.L. Downey, G.E. Galloway, D. John, J. Melillo, J.F. Murley, M.A. O'Neill, M.C. Peacock, B.G. Rabe, and S. Tang. (2010). Building Strong for Tomorrow: NOAA Climate Service.(National Academy of Public Administration, Project Number: 2159-000). Washington, DC: U.S. Department of Commerce, National Oceanic and Atmospheric Administration and the U.S. Congress. Retrieved from http://www.napawash.org/wp-content/uploads/2010/09/NAPA-Final-Report_NOAA-Climate-Service-Study_September-20101.pdf.

Kaushal, S., G. Likens, N. Jaworski, M. Pace, A. Sides, D. Seekell, K. Belt, D. Secor, and R. Wingate. (2010). Rising stream and river temperatures in the United States. Frontiers in Ecology and the Environment 8: 461–466. doi:10.1890/090037.

Keppen, Dan. (2007). Water Supply in a Changing Climate: The Perspective of Family Farmers and Ranchers in the Irrigated West. Family Farm Alliance. Retrieved from http://familyfarmalliance.clubwizard.com/IMUpload/FFA%20Report2.pdf.

Koy, Kevin, S. Van Wart, B. Galey, M. O'Connor, and M. Kely. (2011). CalAdapt: Bringing Global Climate Change Data to a Local Application. Photogrammetric Engineering and Remote Sensing, pp 546-547. Retrieved from: http://cal-adapt.org/.

Kundzewicz, Z.W., L.J. Mata, N.W. Arnell, P. Döll, P. Kabat, B. Jiménez, K.A. Miller, T. Oki, Z. Sen, and I.A. Shiklomanov. (2007). Freshwater Resources and Their Management. In Climate Change 2007: Impacts, Adaptation and Vulnerability. Contribution of Working Group II to the Fourth Assessment Report of the Intergovernmental Panel on Climate Change. [M.L. Parry, O.F. Canziani, J.P. Palutikof, P.J. van der Linden, and C.E. Hanson, (eds.)]. New York: Cambridge University Press. Retrieved from http://www.ipcc.ch/pdf/assessment-report/ar4/wg2/ar4-wg2-chapter3.pdf.

Knowles, N., M.D. Dettinger, and D.R. Cayan. (2006). Trends in Snowfall versus Rainfall in the Western United States. Journal of Climate, 19, 4545-4559.

Lins, Harry F., Robert M. Hirsch, and Julie Kiang. (2010). Water—the Nation's Fundamental Climate Issue: A White Paper on the U.S. Geological Survey Role and Capabilities (Circular

1347). Reston, VA: U.S. Geological Survey. Retrieved from http://pubs.usgs.gov/circ/1347/pdf/circ-1347.pdf.

Milly, P.C.D., J. Betancourt, M. Falkenmark, R.M. Hirsch, Z.W. Kundzewicz, D.P. Lettenmaier, and R.J. Stouffer. (2008). Stationarity is dead: Whither water management? Science, 319, 573–574.

Mimura, N., L. Nurse, R. McLean, J. Agard, L. Briguglio, P. Lefale, R. Payet, and G. Sem. (2007). Small Islands. In Climate Change 2007: Impacts, Adaptation and Vulnerability. Contribution of Working Group II to the Fourth Assessment Report of the Intergovernmental Panel on Climate Change. [M.L. Parry, O.F. Canziani, J.P. Palutikof, P.J. van der Linden, and C.E. Hanson, (eds.)]. New York: Cambridge University Press. Retrieved from http://www.ipcc.ch/pdf/assessment-report/ar4/wg2/ar4-wg2-chapter16.pdf.

Murray, Brian C., W. Aaron Jenkins, Samantha Sifleet, Linwood Pendleton, and Alexis Baldera. (2010). Payments for Blue Carbon: Potential for Protecting Threatened Coastal Habitats. Policy Brief. Nicholas Institute for Environmental Policy Solutions, Duke University. Retrieved from http://nicholasinstitute.duke.edu/oceans/marinees/blue-carbon.

Nabuurs, G.J., O. Masera, K. Andrasko, P. Benitez-Ponce, R. Boer, M. Dutschke, E. Elsiddig, J. Ford-Robertson, P. Frumhoff, T. Karjalainen, O. Krankina, W.A. Kurz, M. Matsumoto, W. Oyhantcabal, N.H. Ravindranath, M.J.S. Sanchez, and X. Zhang. (2007). Forestry. In Climate Change 2007: Mitigation. Contribution of Working Group III to the Fourth Assessment Report of the Intergovernmental Panel on Climate Change. [Metz, B., O. Davidson, P. Bosch, R. Dave, and L. Meyer (eds.)]. New York: Cambridge University Press. Retrieved from http://www.ipcc.ch/pdf/assessment-report/ar4/wg3/ar4-wg3-chapter9.pdf.

National Aeronautics and Space Administration (NASA). (2006). Goddard Institute for Space Studies (GISS) Surface Temperature Analysis. Retrieved from http://www.giss.nasa.gov/research/news/20070208/.

—. (2011). NASA Finds Polar Ice Adding to Rising Seas. Retrieved from http://www.nasa.gov/topics/earth/features/earth20110308.html.

National Association of Clean Water Agencies (NACWA) and Association of Metropolitan Water Agencies (AMWA). (2009). Confronting Climate Change: An Early Analysis of Water and Wastewater Adaptation Costs (Document WBG092409003207DEN). CH2M Hill, Inc, October 2009. Retrieved from http://www.amwa.net/galleries/climate-change/ConfrontingClimateChangeOct09.pdf.

National Oceanic and Atmospheric Administration (NOAA). (2010). National Environmental Satellite, Data, and Information Service (NESDIS)/National Climatic Data Center (NCDC). Retrieved from http://www.ncdc.noaa.gov/oa/ncdc.html.

NOAA/NESDIS/NCDC. (2007). Climate of 2006—in Historical Perspective: Annual Report. Retrieved from http://www.ncdc.noaa.gov/oa/climate/research/2006/ann/ann06.html.

National Research Council of the National Academies. (1999). Global Environmental Change: Research Pathways for the Next Decade. Committee on Global Change Research, Board on Sustainable Development, Policy Division. Washington, DC: National Academy Press.

—. (2004). Adaptive Management for Water Resources Project Planning. Washington, D.C.: National Academy of Sciences. Retrieved from http://www.nap.edu/openbook.php?record_id=10972&page=R2.

—. (2010a). Adapting to the Impacts of Climate Change: America's Climate Choices. Panel on Adapting to the Impacts of Climate Change Board on Atmospheric Sciences and Climate, Division on Earth and Life Sciences, June 22, 2010. Washington D.C: National Academies Press.

—. (2010b). America's Climate Choices. Four Volumes: Limiting the Magnitude of Future Climate Change; Adapting to the Impacts of Climate Change; Advancing the Science of Climate Change; Informing Effective Decisions and Actions Related to Climate Change. Retrieved from http://americasclimatechoices.org/.

Noyes, P.D. M.K. McElweea, H.D. Millera, B.W. Clark, L.A. Van Tiema, K.C. Walcotta, K.N. Erwina, and E.D. Levina. (2009). The Toxicology of Climate Change: Environmental Contaminants in a Warming World. Environment International 35(6), 971-986.

Olsen, R.J., J. Kiang, R. Waskom, (Editors) (2010). Workshop on Nonstationarity, Hydrologic Frequency Analysis, and Water Management (Information Series No. 109). Boulder, CO: Colorado Water Institute. Retrieved from http://www.cwi.colostate.edu.

Proudman Oceanographic Laboratory. Permanent Service for Mean Sea Level (PSMSL), Monthly and Annual Mean Sea Level Station Files. Retrieved from http://www.pol.ac.uk/psmsl/psmsl_individual_stations.html and http://www.pol.ac.uk/psmsl/.

Pulwarty, R.S., D.A. Wilhite, D.M. Diodato, and D.I. Nelson. (2007). Drought in Changing Environments: Creating a Roadmap, Vehicles, and Drivers. Natural Hazards Observer XXXI(5). Boulder, CO: Natural Hazards Center, Institute of Behavioral Science, University of Colorado. Retrieved from http://www.colorado.edu/hazards/o/archives/2007/may07/may07.pdf.

Reardon, D. (1994). Energy Audit Manual for Water/Wastewater Facilities: A Guide for Electric Utilities to Understanding Specific Unit Processes and their Energy/Demand Relationships at Water and Wastewater Plants (EPRI CR-104300). St. Louis, MO: Electric Power Research Institute (EPRI). Retrieved from http://www.epri.com.

Rignot, E., I. Velicogna, M. R. van den Broeke, A. Monaghan, and J. Lenaerts. (2011). Acceleration of the contribution of the Greenland and Antarctic ice sheets to sea level rise. Geophys. Res. Lett., 38, L05503, doi:10.1029/2011GL046583.

Roy, S.B., L. Chen, E. Girvetz, E.P. Maurer, W.B. Mills, and T.M. Grieb. (2010). Evaluating Sustainability of Projected Water Demands Under Future Climate Change Scenarios. Lafayette, CA: Tetra Tech Inc, Prepared for Natural Resources Defense Council. Retrieved from http://rd.tetratech.com/climatechange/projects/doc/Tetra_Tech_Climate_Report_2010_lowres.pdf.

Smith, J.B. (2004). A Synthesis of Potential Climate Change Impacts on the U.S. Pew Center on Global Climate Change. Retrieved from http://www.pewclimate.org/docUploads/Pew-Synthesis.pdf.

Smith, J.B., J.M. Vogel, T.L. Cruce, S. Seidel, and H.A. Holsinger. (2010). Adapting to Climate Change: A Call for Federal Leadership. Pew Center on Global Climate Change. Retrieved from http://www.pewclimate.org/publications/report adapting-to-climate-change-call-for-federal-leadership.

Smith, P., D. Martino, Z. Cai, D. Gwary, H. Janzen, P. Kumar, B. McCarl, S. Ogle, F. O'Mara, C. Rice, B. Scholes, and O. Sirotenko. (2007). Agriculture. In Climate Change 2007: Mitigation. Contribution of Working Group III to the Fourth Assessment Report of the Intergovernmental Panel on Climate Change. [Metz, B., O. Davidson, P. Bosch, R. Dave, and L. Meyer (eds.)]. New York: Cambridge University Press. Retrieved from http://www.ipcc.ch/pdf/assessment-report/ar4/wg3/ar4-wg3-chapter8.pdf.

Spears, M., A. Harrison, V. Sankovich, J. Soddell, and L. Brekke (USGS). (2011). Literature Synthesis on Climate Change Implications for Water and Environmental Resources: Second

Edition. (Technical Memorandum 86-68210-2010-03) Denver, CO: US Bureau of Reclamation Research and Development Office. Retrieved from http://www.usbr.gov/research/docs/climat-echangelitsynthesis.pdf.

Trenberth, K.E., P.D. Jones, P. Ambenje, R. Bojariu, D. Easterling, A. Klein Tank, D. Parker, F. Rahimzadeh, J.A. Renwick, M. Rusticucci, B. Soden, and P. Zhai. (2007). Observations: Surface and Atmospheric Climate Change. In Climate Change 2007: The Physical Science Basis. Contribution of Working Group I to the Fourth Assessment Report of the Intergovernmental Panel on Climate Change. [Solomon, S., D. Qin, M. Manning, Z. Chen, M. Marquis, K.B. Averyt, M. Tignor, and H.L. Miller (eds.)]. New York: Cambridge University Press. Retrieved from http://www.ipcc.ch/pdf/assessment-report/ar4/wg1/ar4-wg1-chapter3.pdf.

University Corporation for Atmospheric Research (UCAR). (2010). National Climate Adaptation Summit Report. National Climate Adaptation Summit, Washington DC, May 25-27. Retrieved from http://www.joss.ucar.edu/events/2010/ncas/ncas_report.pdf.

—. (2008). Advice to the New Administration and Congress: Actions to Make Our Nation Resilient to Severe Weather and Climate Change. Retrieved from http://www.ucar.edu/td/transition.pdf.

U.S. Army Corps of Engineers. (2010). Building Strong Collaborative Relationships for a Sustainable Water Resources Future, National Report: Responding to National Water Resources Challenges. Washington D.C.: U.S. Army Corps of Engineers, Civil Works Directorate. Retrieved from http://www.building-collaboration-for-water.org/Documents/nationalreport_final.pdf

U.S. Bureau of Reclamation. (2011). Addressing Climate Change in Long-Term Water Resources Planning and Management: User Needs for Improving Tools and Information. Retrieved from: http://www.usbr.gov/climate/userneeds/.

U.S. Climate Change Science Program (CCSP). (2007). Effects of Climate Change on Energy Production and Use in the United States (Synthesis and Assessment Product (SAP) 4.5). Retrieved from http://www.climatescience.gov/Library/sap/sap4-5/final-report/sap4-5-final-all.pdf.

—. (2008). Decision Support Experiment and Evaluations Using Seasonal–to-interannual Forecasts and Observational Data: A Focus on Water Resources. Synthesis and Assessment Product 5.3.

U.S. Geological Survey (USGS). (2004). Estimated Use of Water in the United States in 2000 (Circular 1268). Reston, VA: U.S. Geological Survey, U.S. Department of the Interior. Retrieved from http://pubs.usgs.gov/circ/2004/circ1268/.

—. (2010). Water—the Nation's Fundamental Climate Issue: A White Paper on the U.S. Geological Survey Role and Capabilities (Circular 1347). U.S. Department of the Interior.

U.S. Global Change Research Program (USGCRP). (2009). Global Climate Change Impacts in the United States, [Thomas R. Karl, Jerry M. Melillo, and Thomas C. Peterson, (eds.)]. New York: Cambridge University Press. Retrieved from http://www.globalchange.gov/publications/reports/scientific-assessments/us-impacts.

Western States Federal Agency Support Team (WestFAST). (2010). WestFAST Agencies Water-Climate Change Program Inventory, April 2010. Retrieved from http://www.westgov.org/wswc/WestFAST/climate%20change%20inventory%20june%202010%20final.pdf.

White House Council on Environmental Quality. (2010). Progress Report of the Inter-Agency Climate Change Adaptation Task Force: Recommended Actions in Support of a National Climate Change Adaptation Strategy. Retrieved from http://www.whitehouse.gov/sites/default/files/microsites/ceq/Interagency-Climate-Change-Adaptation-Progress-Report.pdf.

World Meteorological Organization (WMO). 2006. Summary Statement on Tropical Cyclones and Climate Change. WMO International Workshop on Tropical Cyclones, IWTC-6, San Jose, Costa Rica, November 2006. Retrieved from. http://www.wmo.ch/pages/prog/arep/tmrp/documents/iwtc_statement.pdf.

APPENDICES A TO F

APPENDIX A

Water Resources and Climate Change Adaptation Workgroup Members

Matthew Larsen (co-chair)	U.S. Geological Survey
Jeff Peterson (co-chair)	Council on Environmental Quality
Mike Shapiro (co-chair)	Environmental Protection Agency
Rolf Olsen	Army Corps of Engineers
Janet Cushing	Army Corps of Engineers
Karl Wirkus	Bureau of Reclamation
Curt Brown	Bureau of Reclamation
Dave Raff	Bureau of Reclamation
Rob Blake	Centers for Disease Control and Prevention
Joan Brunkard	Centers for Disease Control and Prevention
Cathleen Kelly	Council on Environmental Quality
Judsen Bruzgul	Council on Environmental Quality
Christopher Carlson	Department of Agriculture, Forest Service
Noel Gollehon	Department of Agriculture
Allan Hoffman	Department of Energy
Craig Zamuda	Department of Energy
Maria Placht	Department of State
Matt Robinson	Department of State
Karen Metchis	Environmental Protection Agency
Bradley Doorn	National Aeronautics and Space Administration
Nancy Beller-Simms	National Oceanic and Atmospheric Administration
Michael Brewer	National Oceanic and Atmospheric Administration

Priority Action Topic Team Chairs

Water Data Team: Robert Hirsch, U.S. Geological Survey

Vulnerability/Risk Team: Michael Brewer, National Oceanic and Atmospheric Administration

Water Efficiency: Veronica Blette, Environmental Protection Agency

Integrated Water Resources Management: Rolf Olsen, Army Corps of Engineers

Education and Outreach: Joan Brunkard, Centers for Disease Control and Prevention

APPENDIX B

Table of Recommendations and Supporting Actions

Recommendation and Supporting Action	Lead Agency	Implementation (Now or Further Development)	Link to Task Force Progress Report Policy Goals
Recommendation 1 **Establish a Planning Process to Adapt Water Resources Management to a Changing Climate**			
Supporting Action 1: Establish a planning process with the capability to identify priority adaptation actions and promote their implementation	Water Workgroup Co-chairs	Now	Goal 3
Supporting Action 2: Establish an organizational framework to promote effective management of water resources in a changing climate	Water Workgroup Co-chairs	Now	Goal 3
Recommendation 2 **Improve Water Resources and Climate Change Information for Decisionmaking**			
Supporting Action 3: Strengthen data for understanding climate change impacts on water	DOI	Now	Goal 3
Supporting Action 4: Create a formal program to align "hydroclimatic" statistics with today's climate and anticipate future changes	DOI	Now	Goal 3
Supporting Action 5: Implement an active, reliable surveillance system for tracking waterborne diseases and public health threats relevant to climate change	CDC	Further Development	Goal 3
Supporting Action 6: Provide coastal states and communities with essential information to identify areas likely to be inundated by sea level rise	NOAA/USACE	Further Development	Goal 3
Supporting Action 7: Establish interagency effort to expedite implementation of the newly developed wetlands mapping standard	DOI	Now	Goal 3
Recommendation 3 **Strengthen Assessment of Vulnerability of Water Resources to Climate Change**			
Supporting Action 8: Publish guidance on the use of modeled projections for water resources applications	NOAA	Further Development	Goal 2

Recommendation and Supporting Action	Lead Agency	Implementation (Now/Further Development)	Link to Task Force Progress Report Policy Goals
Supporting Action 9: Develop a Federal Internet portal to provide current, relevant, and high quality information on water resources and climate change	NOAA/USACE	Further Development	Goal 2
Supporting Action 10: Develop a pilot climate change vulnerability index for a major category of water facilities and use pilot findings to support vulnerability assessments by other facility categories	NOAA/DOI	Further Development	Goal 2
Supporting Action 11: Continue development of tools and approaches that build capacity for water-related institutions to conduct vulnerability assessments and implement appropriate responses	EPA	Now	Goal 2
Supporting Action 12: Assess vulnerability of watersheds and aquatic systems in National Forests and Grasslands	USDA/Forest Service	Now	Goal 2
Supporting Action 13: Promote free and open access to authoritative climate change science and water resources data	NOAA	Further Development	Goal 2
Recommendation 4 **Expand Water Use Efficiency**			
Supporting Action 14: Develop nationally consistent metrics for water use efficiency in key sectors and report water efficiency information in nationally consistent formats	EPA/USDA/DOE	Now	Goal 3
Supporting Action 15: Consider making water use efficiency an explicit consideration in the revision of Principles and Standards for water resources projects and in the new NEPA guidance on climate change	CEQ	Now	Goal 3
Supporting Action 16: Enhance coordination among Federal water efficiency programs and improve program effectiveness, including creating a "toolbox" of key practices	DOI/EPA/DOE/USACE	Now	Goal 3
Recommendation 5 **Support Integrated Water Resources Management**			
Supporting Action 17: Work with States and interstate bodies (e.g., river basin commissions) to provide assistance needed to incorporate IWRM into their planning and programs, paying particular attention to climate change adaptation issues	USACE	Further Development	Goal 4
Supporting Action 18: Revise Federal water project planning standards to address climate change	CEQ	Now	Goal 3

Recommendation and Supporting Action	Lead Agency	Implementation (Now/Further Development)	Link to Task Force Progress Report Policy Goals
Supporting Action 19: Working with States, review flood risk management planning and drought management planning to identify "best practices" to prepare for hydrologic extremes in a changing climate	USACE	Further Development	Goal 4
Supporting Action 20: Develop benchmarks for incorporating adaptive management into water project designs, operational procedures, and planning strategies	USACE	Now	Goal 3
Recommendation 6 **Support Training and Outreach to Build Response Capability**			
Supporting Action 21: Establish a core training program related to climate change science for local, Tribal, State, and Federal water resources managers	USBR/USACE/NOAA	Now	Goal 3
Supporting Action 22: Focus existing youth outreach programs on climate change and water issues	USDA	Now	Goal 3
Supporting Action 23: Engage Water Resources Research Institutes at land grant colleges and tribal colleges in applied climate change adaptation research and capacity building through annual climate change grant awards	DOI	Further Development	Goal 3
Supporting Action 24: Increase graduate level fellowships in water management and climate change	NOAA	Further Development	Goal 3

APPENDIX C

Selected Interagency Efforts

Project	Scope of Work	Agencies Involved
Climate Science Centers	DOI has begun to establish eight regional Climate Science Centers (CSCs) that will synthesize existing climate change impact data and management strategies, help resource managers put them into action on the ground, and engage the public through education.	DOI and other agencies
Landscape Conservation Cooperatives	As part of its strategy to address climate change at the local and regional level, DOI is creating twenty-one Landscape Conservation Cooperatives (LCCs).	DOI and other agencies
National Integrated Drought Information System (NIDIS)	The goal of NIDIS is to improve the Nation's capacity to proactively manage drought-related risks, by providing those affected with the best available information and tools to assess the potential impacts of drought, and to better prepare for and mitigate the effects of drought.	DOC (NOAA), USDA, DOE, USACE, EPA, DOI (USGS, USBR), DOT, FERC, FCA, IRS, USITC, NASA, NSF, SBA
NOAA Regional Integrated Sciences and Assessment (RISAs)	The RISA program supports research that addresses complex climate sensitive issues of concern to decision-makers and policy planners at a regional level.	NOAA and other agencies
Climate Change and Water Working Group (CCAWWG)	CCAWWG is a joint effort by principal water resources management agencies and the earth science data collection agencies of the U.S. Government.	USGS, NOAA, USBR, USACE, EPA, NASA, FEMA
Western States Federal Agency Support Team (WESTFAST)	WESTFAST provides support to Western States Water Council to implement the Western Governors Association report, "Water Needs and Strategies for a Sustainable Future: Next Steps."	USACE, EPA, USGS, USBR, NOAA, NRCS, USFS, USFWS, BLM, DOE

Activities and Adaptation Assets	Adaptation Programmatic Needs and Opportunities
• CSCs are being developed in coordination with other Federal agencies, local and state partners, and the public.	• CSCs will coordinate with RISAs and anticipate using model results and projections produced by RISA-supported scientists.
• The LCCs are to coordinate landscape-level strategies for conserving public lands, wildlife, water and other natural resources. Some of the LCC products and services will include computer models, projections of species' ranges with climate change, assessments of species' and landscapes' vulnerability to climate change and maps showing potential wildlife movement corridors as climate change forces migration. Each of the LCCs is created for a specific landscape type, with boundaries that cross both state lines and international borders.	• LCCs are to collaborate with academia, other Federal agencies, local and state partners, and the public and will coordinate with CSCs and RISAs in their regions.
• U.S. Drought Portal is an interactive system to: provide early warning about emerging and anticipated droughts; assimilate quality control data about droughts and models; provide information about risk and impact of droughts to different agencies and stakeholders; provide information about past droughts for comparison and to understand current conditions; explain how to plan for and manage the impacts of droughts; provide a forum for different stakeholders to discuss drought-related issues.	• Develop leadership and networks to implement an integrated drought monitoring and forecasting system at Federal, State, and local levels. • Foster and support a research focusing on risk assessment, forecasting, and management. • Create a drought "early warning system" to provide accurate, timely, and integrated information. • Develop interactive systems, such as the Web Portal, as part of the early warning system. • Provide a framework for public awareness and education about droughts.
• RISA research team members work closely with natural resource managers and land planners, nongovernmental organizations and the private sector within each region to advance new research on how climate variability and change will impact the environment, economy, and society, and develop innovative ways to integrate climate information into decision-making.	• Research topics include fisheries, water, wildfire, agriculture, public health and coastal restoration. Team members are primarily based at universities though some of the team members are based at government research facilities, non-profit organizations or private sector entities.
• CCAWWG produced Climate Change and Water Resources Management: A Federal Perspective with strategies to improve water management by tracking, anticipating, and responding to climate effects. CCAWWG is developing a comprehensive capability assessment and research plan that supports the common and complementary needs of the Federal and non-Federal water management community.	• Work with Federal and non-Federal research programs to find ways for their programs to assist in implementing the research plan and to generate collaborative research efforts across members of the water management and scientific communities to close these gaps.
• Coordination of Federal activities in the Western States to support multiple climate change adaptation activities.	• Continue and expand funding for data collection networks and activities necessary for monitoring, assessing, and predicting future water supplies. • Research for improving the predictive capabilities for climate change, and assessment and mitigation of its impacts.

Selected Interagency Efforts (continued)

Project	Scope of Work	Agencies involved
Integrated Water Resources Science and Services (IWRSS)	Federal agency partnership working toward an integrative water resources information system.	NOAA, USACE, USGS
Joint Climate Prediction Research Program	Development of climate system models more powerful than existing models.	DOE, USDA, NSF
Border Region Cooperative Efforts	Individual and joint efforts by the United States, Mexico and Canada to assess, study and propose responses to the impact of climate change on water management on the border and within transboundary lakes and river basins.	USGS, NOAA, USBR,

Activities and Adaptation Assets	Adaptation Program Opportunities
• Envisions a highly collaborative and integrative framework for providing a seamless suite of water resources information across scales ranging from small hillslopes to large watersheds, from droughts to floods, and from historical analyses to long–range predictions.	———
• High resolution models are being developed for predicting climate change and its resulting impacts at more localized scales and over shorter time periods than previously possible.	• Program designed to generate models, significantly more powerful than existing models, that can help decisionmakers develop adaptation strategies addressing climate change. • Efforts will provide improved capability with improved geographical and temporal resolution.
• Climate and water–related components of EPA's Border Environment Program (Border 2012) with Mexico • Flood Warning and Discharge Monitoring project undertaken by USGS in Nogales, Arizona/ Nogales, Sonora • IBWC and BOR joint cooperative efforts with Mexican counterparts in the Colorado River basin on behalf of water conservation, new sourcing, and environmental uses • New annex on Climate Change Impacts to be included in revised Great Lakes Water Quality Agreement (currently being renegotiated) • International Joint Commission's International Upper Great Lakes Study Board will examine potential climate change impacts on Lake Superior and Lake Huron and propose measures for adaptation.	• Enhance the focus of research and monitoring efforts on transboundary water/climate issues. • Seek opportunities for consistent coordination and cooperation among Federal, state–level and academic research programs to generate the fullest possible collaboration among relevant water management and scientific communities. • Increase binational collaboration on quantifying and understanding impacts of climate change in Great Lakes and the Colorado and Rio Grande river basins. • Coordinate adaptation strategies to reduce climate change risks to the Colorado and Rio Grande river basins and the Great Lakes, and increase resilience of respective aquatic ecosystems.

Selected Agency Activities

Agency	Scope of Water-Climate Work	Adaptation Activities
DOE	• Ensure a reliable energy supply; • Meet the energy requirements for water use; • Manage water needs for energy production; and • Develop water-efficient environmentally sustainable energy-related technologies.	• Assessed major water issues related to electrical generation and transportation fuels production, and the potential impact of climate change • Identified approaches that could reduce freshwater use in the energy sector including: (1) energy efficiency improvements in homes, buildings, industry and transportation; (2) use of non-traditional water sources including water reuse; and (3) optimizing energy production to reduce water intensity. • Produced "Energy Demands on Water Resources" • Participating agency in multiple forums, including: USGCRP; SWAQ, and WestFAST
USGS	• Provide reliable, impartial and timely scientific information to understand the earth; serve as the primary Federal science agency for water resource information in the 21st century; provide science information to decision-makers	• Produced "Climate change and water resources management: A Federal perspective" with strategies to improve water management by tracking, anticipating, and responding to climate effects • Making long-term monitoring networks available to establish baselines, calibrate/validate models, and support and evaluate adaptation strategies • Producing stream flow forecasts with NOAA
NOAA	• Provide reliable, unbiased science products and services for citizens, planners, emergency managers, and other decisionmakers; produce climate and weather forecasts and severe storm warnings for the safety of life and property; conduct climate monitoring; manage fisheries and endangered species and their habitat; support coastal habitat restoration and marine commerce	• Leading efforts to improve the nation's response and adaptation to and mitigation of drought through the National Integrated Drought Information System (NIDIS) which serves as a model for climate services • Forecasting water-related climatic variables (e.g., precipitation and soil moisture); stream flow and western snowpack (with USDA); • Updating precipitation duration/frequency atlases of recent decades of observations; • Maintaining mitigation and adaptation clearinghouses such as the Coastal Climate Adaptation which contain guides, plans, tools, and education materials • Participate in interagency USGCRP, which supports research on climate and associated global changes. • Providing authors and lead authors to the Intergovernmental Panel on Climate Change assessments • Providing authors and lead authors to the National Fish, Wildlife, and Plants Climate Adaptation Strategy (co-lead with the U.S. Fish and Wildlife Service and the state wildlife agencies)
USACE	• Manage flood risk, navigation, hydropower, water supply, and infrastructure and practice environmental stewardship; provide emergency response; reduce damage of floods and mitigate impacts of drought	• Revised guidance on how to incorporate future sea-level change projections into life cycle of USACE projects
CDC	• Serve as the Nation's lead public health agency to conduct and support research on health effects related to climate change; monitor, detect, and prevent waterborne disease in the United States; provide technical assistance and funding to local, State, and territorial health departments; provide scientific data on climate-related health outcomes to decisionmakers	• Maintaining a national database of all waterborne outbreaks reported in the United States • Providing grants to States and cities to address and prepare for the health effects related to climate change as part of CDC's Climate Ready States and Cities Initiative. • Researching the water and public health impacts of climate change • Developing national guidance on the public health implications of drought

Potential Water Adaptation Assets	Adaptation Programmatic Needs and Opportunities
• Super-computing resources and modeling capabilities to assess potential climate change impacts on water resources and energy production. • National labs—research and technology development • Broad range of research and development activities at universities, at DOE National Laboratories, and in cooperative agreements with the private sector	• Improve regional/local scale forecasts of climate change • Conduct full assessment of risks and impacts of climate change on existing energy sector infrastructure • Develop technologies and practices for reducing and recovering from climate change impacts on water resources either requiring energy or used in energy production
• Robust monitoring network • Hydrologic expertise • Long-run datasets	• Develop paleoclimate information and stochastic modeling as useful tools for developing climate scenarios that include a wide range of potential hydroclimatic conditions • Adopt a System Projection paradigm (rather than a Stationary System paradigm) for adaptation planning • Improve groundwater monitoring • Coordinate with USGS-led interagency effort on water security
• Extensive regional and local infrastructure for delivering climate information and mitigation/adaptation support including NWS Forecast Offices, Regional Integrated Sciences and Assessment universities, Regional Climate Centers, Sea Grant, State Climatologists, and others. • Production of climate change scenarios • Delivery of coastal climate adaptation and mitigation information (e.g., sea level rise and inundation) through the Coastal Services Center and Sea Grant; consideration of climate change impacts when providing comments on other Federal agencies' proposed actions that could affect essential fish habitat or endangered species	• Establish NOAA's National Climate Service • Strengthen weather and climate observations and monitoring at the regional and local levels (includes modernizing the Historical Climate Network and the Cooperative Observer Network) • Improve climate scenario models and short-term forecasts; build bridges between the two • Improve the downscaling of climate models and assessments • Fill need for increased financial resources; • Funding to complete updating of precipitation/duration/frequency atlases and to develop revised methods for engineering use for long-term infrastructure design.
• National Flood Risk Management Program • Federal Interagency Floodplain Management Task Force (co-lead with FEMA) • Risk-informed decision making guidance and procedures	• Address key knowledge gaps • Monitor climate, hydrology, and ecosystems • Develop planning methods to account for climate uncertainty and facilitate adaptation
• Surveillance System and national database of all waterborne outbreaks reported in the United States • CDC's Climate Ready States and Cities Initiative • National Environmental Public Health Tracking Network • Strong relationships with health departments at State and local levels to coordinate adaptation efforts and activities • Environmental Health Training for Emergency Response course to help local health departments prepare for natural disasters	• Develop and maintain robust surveillance systems for climate-sensitive diseases (e.g., waterborne disease and mosquito-borne disease) so that long-term datasets are available for analysis and future planning • Increase investment in monitoring, detecting, and preventing waterborne disease at local, State, and national levels • Provide resources and training to local health departments to respond to climate-related public health emergencies (e.g., floods, hurricanes, extreme weather events) • Strengthen climate change and health research, programmatic activities, and workforce at Federal, State, and local levels-

Selected Agency Activities (continued)

Agency	Scope of Water-Climate Work	Adaptation Activities
NASA	• Study the Earth system from space as part of the scientific discovery mission; create new space-based and related capabilities to advance scientific understanding and enhance civil space-based Earth observation; conduct water cycle research and application development	• Producing downscaled climate models and assessing the uncertainty of these models • Improved water models by increasing the access to Earth observations • Collaborating with State, Tribal and local water managers • Engaging in US drought and disaster interagency and independent efforts • Water Cycle research program and Water Resources application program provides funding to researchers to integrate water impacts of climate change using models, aerial, and space observations
USDA	• Ensure the sustainability of food and fiber production for consumption by the American public and export around the world; prepare for water related climate impacts that threaten US agriculture; proactively manage for watershed resilience and enhance the adaptability of forest ecosystems to protect those ecosystems' ability to provide clean water	• Partnering with research and development collaborators to advance understanding, quantification and prediction of climate change effects on agricultural and forest systems • Developing knowledge and tools to enhance the ability of conservation systems and practices to mitigate climate change effects • Developing and providing for outreach to internal and external stakeholders to assist in decision-making related to climate change on agricultural lands • Providing technical assistance to States, local governments and Tribes for natural resource studies and plans for watershed protection, flood prevention, irrigation, drainage, rural water supply, etc. • Creating and cultivating effective partnerships to promote collaborative actions across larger landscapes to increase awareness of the critical role of healthy forested watersheds
Bureau of Reclamation	• Assist in meeting the increasing water demands of the West; protect the environment; protect public's investment in water infrastructure	• Assessing changes in water flows on Federal lands • Assessing changing water needs as a result of climate impacts • Working to determine how flood events will change and impact Federal lands under a changing climate • WaterSMART Basin Study Program
EPA	• Develop national programs, regulation, policies and technical guidance to protect the quality and integrity of the nation's drinking water, surface water, groundwater, and marine water resources	• Produced "2008 National Water Program Strategy: Response to Climate Change" and the subsequent "2010 NWP: Key Action Update" to understand implications of climate change for clean water and drinking water programs and implemented 44 Key Actions throughout the base program, as well as in EPA Regions; currently updating strategy • Climate Ready Estuaries Program works with the National Estuaries Programs to develop and implement adaptation tools. • Climate Ready Water Utilities program works with the drinking water, wastewater and stormwater management utilities to develop and promote methods for understanding and reducing risk to climate change. • WaterSense water efficiency program partners with private sector to advance water efficient products and practices. • Participating Agency in USGCRP and lead author on several reports. • Active R&D program evaluating impacts and effects of environmental stressors on human health and the environment, including climate change; tests new technologies and practices, including for water infrastructure, nonpoint source controls, etc.
FEMA	• Support citizens and first responders to build, sustain, and improve capabilities to prepare for, protect against, respond to, recover from, and mitigate all hazards	• Conducting a study on the impact of climate change on the National Flood Insurance Program (NFIP) • Revising FEMA's Coastal Construction Manual to include recommendations concerning coastal construction siting and design within the context of potential climate change impacts • Studying the physics that drive natural hazard processes and severity to develop innovative measures for reducing damage resulting from such hazards • Studying mission and resource requirements associated with expanded operational demands due to climate change impacts

Potential Water Adaptation Assets	Adaptation Programmatic Needs and Opportunities
• Longest continuous record of the Earth's surface (Landsat) • Earth Observing System (EOS) with global data on the State of the atmosphere, land, and oceans • Earth science research and applied science to establish baselines, forecasts, and risk • Global Precipitation Mission with Japan Aerospace Exploration Agency and others	• Respond to increased demand for data products, downscaled predictive models, imagery, etc. • Initiate planned Soil Moisture Active-Passive (SMAP) to take direct measurements of soil moisture and freeze/thaw state to improve understanding of water cycles and forecasts for weather, flood, drought, and agricultural productivity • Manage risk of critical data and monitoring gaps due to aging space-based missions and lag-times for replacement
• Financial and technical assistance to farmers and ranchers who face natural resource threats, with priority given to water conservation or irrigation efficiency applications • Work with public and private partners to support entrepreneurial watershed management projects and to promote adaptive management	• Develop new methods, tools, and assessment protocols to evaluate the effectiveness of current and future conservation systems and practices for increasingly variable climatic conditions • Conduct research to identify or develop more drought resistant crops and trees, gather information to support a better understanding of interactions between climate and ecosystems to evaluate management options, and test solutions • Redesign our current water storage and management infrastructure • Revitalize programs such as the Small Watershed Program and build networks of small dams to manage water flow to respond to changes in water quantity • Capture data to adequately describe current conditions and produce models to develop site specific planning thresholds to inform decisionmakers and the public on the scope of the impacts
• Paleoclimate information and stochastic data for expanding the range of hydrologic variability considered	• Access additional information on climate-water impacts through literature, projections, data, and planning scenarios • Improve the ability to assess social systems response to climate change • Establish practices for assessing operations and resource responses • Develop the ability to assess, characterize, and communicate uncertainties
• State-Tribal Climate Change Council (STC3) involving governmental co-regulators to develop adaptation strategies • National Tribal Water Council facilitates working with Tribal government water professionals • Research capability to conduct studies on human health and the environment, and to develop and test adaptation methods for water infrastructure, watershed management, nonpoint source controls, and aquatic systems • Many stakeholder partnerships, including Green Infrastructure initiative; Sourcewater Collaborative; Effective Utility Management partnership; WaterSense and Sustainable Infrastructure program	• Baseline and monitoring data on shifting background parameters of water quality, water flow, temperature, and aquatic habitat to support climate-corrected policies and engineering design standards (e.g., 7Q10 flow, 25-year 24-hour rainfall, 100-year storm, etc.) • Methods for projecting local hydrological shifts for long-term infrastructure planning, to prepare for increased risk of high flow and high velocity events due to intense storms as well as potential low flow periods • Technical assistance and guidance for States, Tribes, municipalities, and watershed groups • Guidance and decision tools, especially for small-to-medium sized drinking and waste water utilities • Definitions for most water efficient technologies (MET) for sector of expertise, (e.g., EPA for domestic water use; DOE for power plants, and USDA for agriculture.

APPENDIX D

Summary of Public Comments

Given the broad and diverse array of stakeholders in water resources management, input from the public was deemed critical to development of the National Action Plan. The Water Resources and Climate Change Adaptation Workgroup created multiple avenues throughout the planning process to collaborate with and receive feedback from the public. Public input and feedback were solicited through a series of stakeholder "listening sessions" in 2009 and 2011 and by written comments on the draft Plan released for public comment in early June 2011.

Participants at listening sessions expressed views and perspectives on a wide range of climate-related issues affecting water resources. Participants included organizations that are knowledgeable about the impacts of a changing climate on freshwater resources and engaged in water resources management and representatives and leaders of environmental organizations, river basin commissions, public health organizations, trade associations, utility associations, State and local planning and management agencies, Tribes, and representatives from energy, industry, and transportation. A list of some of the organizations that participated in the listening sessions is provided at the end of this Appendix. The Workgroup also received written comments from both organizations and individuals through online submissions.

Feedback from the listening sessions and online comments offered a valuable resource to the Workgroup, ensuring that the final report and plan were inclusive of many perspectives, experiences, and concerns of each constituency, as well as providing a channel to buttress the report with demonstrations of successful local, state, and regional policies and programs to consider as part of a national strategy.

Many comments provided early in the process in 2009 served either to confirm or guide the direction of recommendations undertaken by the Workgroup. For example, issues raised in the first group of listening sessions regarding IWRM and floodplain management, long-term monitoring needs, and collaborative planning were built into the drafting of the report. Comments provided later in the process on the draft Plan served to strengthen the final Plan. More information concerning comments is provided below.

Listening Sessions and Public Comments—Summer 2011

The Workgroup released a draft of the National Action Plan for public comment in early June 2011, soliciting comments from the general public, through online comment submissions, and from stakeholder organizations including:

- State, Tribal, and local governments and water utilities;
- energy, industry, and transportation associations;
- environmental organizations; and
- agricultural organizations.

Through four listening sessions, hosted by Federal agencies key to the implementation of the report, and the written comments received between June 2 and July 15, 2011, a number of consistent themes emerged. The Workgroup has addressed these ideas in the final Plan to the extent possible.

Support for strengthening existing collaborative planning efforts

Many commenters supported the Plan's focus on strengthening collaboration among the community of Federal agencies, non-governmental organizations, and the research community and the decision not to establish major new organizations or programs.

Strengthen infrastructure planning for changing extremes

Comments received in the review of the draft Plan encouraged greater recognition of the importance of strengthening planning for water infrastructure. Several commenters recommended that the Plan also give greater attention to expanded use of "green infrastructure" practices. Other commenters recommended expanded attention to the value of dams to better manage more variable water resources.

Improve understanding of climate change impacts on aquatic ecosystems and watersheds

Many of the tools and collaborations being developed are focused on protection of infrastructure or water supply. More attention needs to be paid to understanding the effects of climate change on natural systems and developing strategies for improving their resilience.

Affirm the principle of integrated water resources management (IWRM)

Many comments affirmed the Plan's recommendation to address climate and water challenges in the context of IWRM. IWRM, many participants agreed, is a critical organizing principle for managing scarce and fluctuating water resources across many sectors and users.

Expand Federal support for State, Tribal, and local climate adaptation

Commenters stressed the importance of water data and information, including reliable predictive models of future conditions, to support effective State, Tribal, and local adaptation decisions. In addition, many States, Tribes, regions, and localities are already implementing their own adaptation planning processes and Federal efforts toward managing freshwater resources in a changing climate should include expanded efforts to partner with, learn from, and improve these activities, especially those related to climate change education.

Concern over sufficiency of recommended response actions in the context of challenges

Some commenters expressed concern that the proposed recommendations and supporting actions were needed, but not sufficient to accomplish a significant shift in methods and approaches to water resources management suggested by projected changes in climate and water resources.

Protect indigenous communities

The Workgroup also heard from representatives of Tribal nations that indigenous people are subject to a range of challenges related to a changing climate. Many of these communities have observed climate-related changes that are already underway. Listening session participants stressed that these effects are not simply "changes" to be adapted to—they represent a fundamental crisis of survival for communities' livelihoods and cultures.

Listening Sessions—Fall 2009

The Workgroup convened a series of six listening sessions with stakeholder organizations in October and December 2009 to solicit input early in the planning process. The Workgroup invited participants across interested sectors, holding targeted listening sessions with individuals representing the following interests:

- energy and industrial organizations;
- State, Tribal, local governments;

- water utility organizations;
- environmental and coastal organizations;
- agriculture and transportation organizations; and
- public health organizations.

These listening sessions provided a forum for interested parties to voice their views on water resources and risks posed by climate change early in the Workgroup's process and to build those views and related concerns, questions, and suggestions into the report. These comments helped to lay the foundation for the priorities for water resources management in a changing climate addressed by the report.

Major themes addressed in the scope of the initial listening sessions included:

Crosscutting impacts of a changing climate on water resources infrastructure

Because many of the impacts of climate change will be borne by water (in the form of changing patterns and extreme events), so will a changing climate deeply impact the many facets of commercial, industrial, and cultural life, as well as ecosystems, dependent until now upon historical and stationary norms of water availability and quality. Participants voiced the concern that, as these climate patterns shift, sometimes unpredictably and sometimes as extreme events, infrastructure planning must take into account not only the impacts on individual sectors, users, and issues, but on many interrelated ones. The consistent availability of water for many decades, for example, is critical to the function of much of the Nation's energy infrastructure, and future energy planning must consider the availability of water resources. Failure to address these stressors together presents a significant risk to public health, safety, and the economic and daily quality of life of communities. Many of these comments helped to frame recommendations to establish a planning process and organizational framework for water resources planning, to improve water use efficiency, and to support IWRM.

Facilitating integrated planning for diverse users, needs, and challenges

Participants in the sessions represented a diverse community of water uses and of vulnerabilities to changing water resources. Policymakers and water resource managers face issues of concern, including how to balance traditional water rights with scarce resources in periods of drought; how to monitor and coordinate groundwater and surface water withdrawals across sectors; promoting water reuse and efficiency; building strategies for effective floodplain management in areas vulnerable to increased precipitation; and how to meet the needs of vulnerable populations that already face water-related and other challenges around health, safety, food security, housing, education, and economy. The development and expansion of integrated water resources management (IWRM) policies will be critical to ensuring that the needs of all users are adequately satisfied and that vulnerable communities are secured. Participants noted that coordination of water resource adaptation planning with other planning efforts will require integrated approaches that are multi-media, cross-sectoral, and watershed-based and that take into account the "triple bottom line" of economy, ecology, and social goals. Many of these comments and concerns were built into recommendations to strengthen vulnerability assessments and support IWRM.

Improve Federal planning, agency coordination, and data monitoring and access

Participants at these listening sessions voiced the need for an organized Federal planning structure to respond to climate-water challenges. Participants affirmed the need for an organizational framework and planning process, expressed in Actions 1 and 2, and the need to better coordinate existing Federal programs and initiatives for water resources planning and management. Members of many stakeholder communities also advocated the need for improved and expanded scientific monitoring networks and capabilities, improved data interoperability, and free public access to data. The Federal government can also work to develop tools to communicate data and diffuse water management policies, and best practices for planners and decisionmakers. These are foundational components to a successful long-term planning process that is at once transparent and based on comprehensive and sound science.

Facilitate collaborative adaptation planning and provide education opportunities

Because climate impacts on water resources will vary, depending on local topography, regional climate systems, watersheds, and water-use demographics, participants expressed the importance of a collaborative planning process between Federal agencies and State, Tribal, local watershed, and other decision-making bodies. Federal efforts toward this end can include more detailed local and region-specific data-monitoring networks, helping build capacity, diffusing best practices, and creating partnerships while allowing State and local authorities the flexibility to make decisions within their communities. Furthermore, participants voiced the need for expanding programs to build local knowledge and capacity and to educate both the public and decisionmakers about the challenges and solutions to water-resources management in a changing climate.

Selected Participating Organizations

The following is a list of selected organizations that offered feedback through the listening sessions and online comment period. This list is by no means exhaustive but serves to illustrate the diversity of stakeholders whose input was considered in the final drafting of the report.

American Association of State Highway Transportation Officials

American Rivers

American Society of Agronomy

American Society of Civil Engineers

American Sportfishing Association

Association of California Water Agencies

Association of State and Interstate Water Pollution Control Administrators

Association of State Drinking Water Administrators

Association of State Wetlands Managers

Chevron Corporation

Delaware River Basin Commission

Denver Water

Edison Electric Institute

Energetics, Inc.

Family Farm Alliance

Interstate Council on Water Policy

Idaho National Laboratories

National Association of Clean Water Agencies

National Groundwater Association

Natural Resources Defense Council

Oregon Water Resources Congress

Pennsylvania Fish and Boat Commission

WaterCat Consulting

Waterways Council

Wills and Carlson, LLP

APPENDIX E

Overview of Water Resource Management Decisions

Types of decisions	Who makes them	Examples of scientific information needed to support decisions
Investments in future water supply and water use infrastructure	Cities, farmers, energy companies, utilities municipal governments, Federal agencies	Streamflow and groundwater recharge Water demand (by crops, or energy production system, or people)
Permits for discharge of wastewater or other pollutants and underground injection programs	EPA, State, and Tribal environmental agencies	Low-flow characteristics of rivers (discharge, temperature, pollutant loadings) Properties of underground sources of drinking water
Design of water and energy facilities near sea level (including water supplies; water storage and distribution systems; wastewater collection, reclamation and reuse; irrigators, power plants that rely on water; stormwater management)	Cities, farmers, industry, utilities, municipal, State, local, Federal, and Tribal governments	Estimates of relative sea level rise and storm-surge hazard
Inland flood hazard mitigation	Property owners, municipal and Tribal governments, transportation planners and operators, insurance industry	Flood frequency estimates
Design and rehabilitation of urban and rural drainage systems, including new "green" infrastructure	Municipal and Tribal governments, transportation authorities	Estimates of the magnitude, frequency, and duration of extreme rainfall and small-stream flooding
Operation of water infrastructure (dams and diversions) at time scales from hours to years	Owners and operators of that infrastructure, including Federal, State, municipal, and Tribal agencies and energy companies	Estimates of the probability and magnitude of extreme low flows and extreme flood flows and flood volumes Estimates of water demand, forecasts at multiple time scales of the amount of inflow Estimates of the consequences of various flow scenarios on aquatic habitats
Protecting public health from waterborne disease	Public water supply utilities, public health officials, EPA and State and Tribal environmental agencies	Reliable data on waterborne disease incidence in populations Estimates of the likely timing and location of water-borne pathogens and contaminants Monitoring systems and interventions for reducing health impacts
Protecting or restoring aquatic and riparian habitats	Many agencies at the Federal, State, Tribal, or local level	Estimates of the likely streamflow at multiple times and scales, water temperature, water quality, and variability, as well as how those conditions will affect habitat and biological populations

APPENDIX F

Examples of Risk Assessment Tools

Example: USACE Dam Safety Action Classification (DSAC)

The USACE Dam Safety Action Classification (DSAC) is a method used by the USACE to manage dam safety risk. The program ensures that all dams and appurtenant structures are designed, constructed, and operated safely and effectively under all conditions on the basis of the dam safety program purposes, as adopted by the Interagency Committee on Dam Safety.

DSAC Categories:

Class I: Urgent and Compelling—Critically Near Failure OR Extremely High Risk

Class II: Urgent—Failure Initiation Foreseen OR Very High Risk

Class III: High Priority—Significantly Inadequate OR Moderate to High Risk

Class IV: Priority—Inadequate with Low Risk

Class V: Normal—Adequately Safe AND Residual Risk is Considered Tolerable

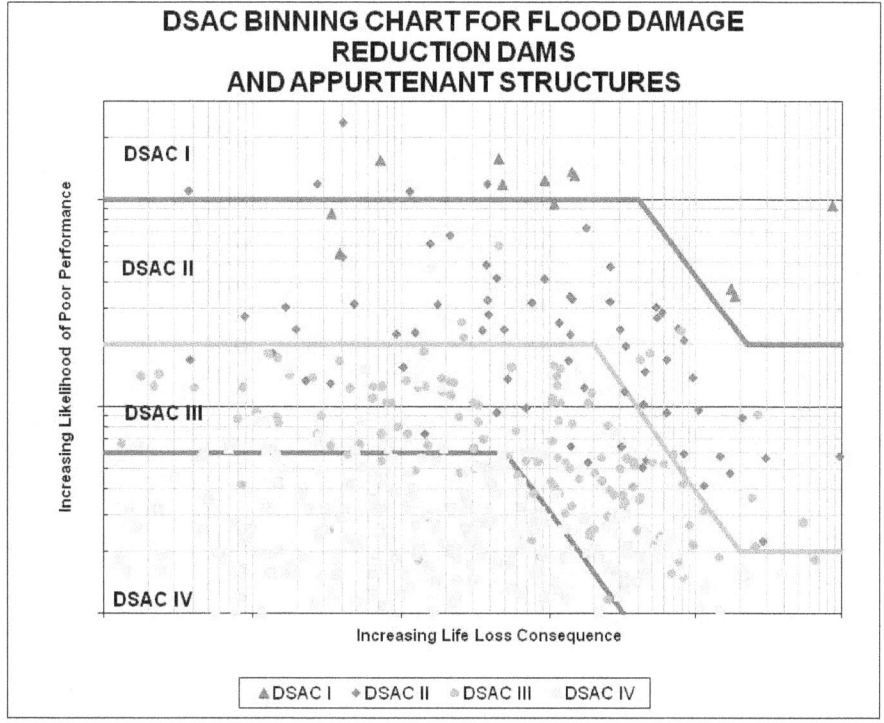

The graph above plots dams on the likelihood of failure of the structure and the potential loss of life as a result. Vulnerability assessments of aquatic ecosystems and water resources infrastructure, such as wastewater facilities and dams, can use this comparison to prioritize projects. Consequences of failure can also be framed in terms of economic losses and environmental/ecosystem losses, among others, and presented on the x-axis. Limited resources can be focused on high priority projects using this matrix.

Example: NOAA Roadmap for Adapting to Coastal Risk

Community planning provides an opportunity to address hazards and climate change vulnerabilities, because residents and other stakeholders are already creating or updating policies and plans that will guide community development. Decisions are being made on land use, government services, community character, and natural resource protection. Hazards are connected to all these sectors and affect operations and budgets.

The NOAA Coastal Services Center developed the Roadmap for Adapting to Coastal Risk, which is a participatory process for assessing a community's vulnerability to hazards and for incorporating relevant data and information about hazards and climate into ongoing local planning and decisionmaking.

The Roadmap for Adapting to Coastal Risk approach emphasizes the importance of viewing community planning and development decisions through a hazards and climate lens. This means identifying how hazards and climate change can intensify existing issues, such as stormwater management and infrastructure maintenance. This participatory assessment process is designed to:

- Engage key staff members and stakeholders in a comprehensive, yet rapid, assessment of local vulnerabilities;
- Use existing information resources to evaluate potential hazard and climate impacts;
- Collaborate across disciplines to better understand and plan for impacts; and
- Identify opportunities for improving resilience to current and future hazard risks.

A three-hour training introduces the "Roadmap" assessment methodology. Visit the Roadmap Web site www.csc.noaa.gov/roadmap to learn more.

Example: Vulnerability Assessment Guide and Training (DOI, NOAA, and NWF)

New guidelines have been developed to help natural resources professionals understand how the changing climate is likely to affect fish and wildlife and the habitats on which they depend. Training for applying the guidelines is paramount to designing and carrying out effective adaptation strategies to counter the impacts of climate change. NOAA is contributing to work by the U.S. Department of the Interior and the National Wildlife Federation (NWF) to train managers to develop and use vulnerability assessments as part of their broader adaptation planning efforts for freshwater, coastal, and inland ecosystems. Training workshops are being designed, based on the new document, "Scanning the Conservation Horizon: A Guide to Climate Change Vulnerability Assessment," developed jointly by the National Wildlife Federation, State and Federal agencies, and other partners.

Vulnerability assessments are a key step in adaptation planning by enabling managers to:

- Identify those species and habitats most likely to be in need of conservation actions as a result of climate change;
- Develop adaptation strategies tailored for managing species and habitats in greatest need;
- Foster collaboration at statewide and regional scales by providing a shared understanding of impacts and management options; and
- Allow scarce resources for wildlife and habitat conservation to be allocated efficiently in the face of climate change.

Example: EPA Climate Resilience Evaluation and Awareness Tool

In response to actionable signals indicating localized climate impacts that hold the potential to affect operational conditions, a drinking water or wastewater (water sector) utility would conduct an assessment of climate impact risks (vulnerabilities, threats, and consequences) looking at a broad range of potential systems implications. This focused engagement would include assessing the risk of a range of water-sector-system component responses to climate change-related watershed variation. A climate change risk assessment would be used to evaluate the overall risk to water systems of climate impacts.

Two alternative, though potentially complimentary, approaches to risk analysis have been articulated—"top-down" (quantitative scenario risk approach) and "bottom-up" (qualitative threshold risk assessment). The quantitative scenario risk approach seeks to employ "downscaled" outputs of general circulation climate models as inputs to localized hydrologic and other models to simulate a range of water-sector-system component responses to climate-change-related watershed variation. Bottom-up approaches draw on the general findings of climate research, with utilities identifying system components potentially dependent on the status of key climate variables (e.g., temperature and precipitation) resulting in a preliminary risk assessment based on the professional judgment of experts who know the system and local watershed conditions. In response to risk assessment outputs, a water sector utility would develop strategies to address the identified risk, including expanded operating flexibility, expanded capacity, and development of alternative supply and treatment options.

As a result of the issues identified above, the U.S. Environmental Protection Agency has developed a computer-based Climate Resilience Evaluation and Awareness Tool (CREAT) for drinking water and wastewater utility owners and operators under its Climate Ready Water Utilities Program. The first version of CREAT is available for download at the Climate Ready Water Utilities Website (http://water.epa.gov/infrastructure/watersecurity/climate/creat.cfm). The second version of CREAT, which is currently under development, will incorporate the top-down as well as the bottom-up risk assessment approaches and will use the most current scientific understanding of climate change. The tool will assist water sector utility owners and operators in understanding potential climate change threats and in assessing the related risks at their individual utilities.

Individual utilities can analyze climate change as part of adaptation planning by using forecasts of future climate at a regional scale. However, the art of climate modeling is evolving and is not fully understood. Model resolution is coarse and there is often substantial variability across climate models (mainly concerning precipitation projections). There is a critical need to conduct planning and make engineering and management decisions regardless of the considerable uncertainties about the timing, location and scale of future climate impacts. For most utilities, there is not an option to "wait and see" or take no action. Both the current stock of capital assets and any new investments will be affected by climate change, even if the impacts cannot be precisely predicted. Thus, there is a need for an approach that can be used by utilities now to understand and evaluate potential adaptation measures.

CREAT allows water sector utility owners and operators to use known information about their utility, such as utility assets, to assist with identifying climate change threats, assessing potential consequences, and evaluating adaptation options. This approach allows users to help establish the thresholds at which climate change threats could result in asset or mission failure and to initiate adaptation planning despite the uncertainties. CREAT may also help organize and communicate climate-related activities to decisionmakers, stakeholders, and citizens. This may build confidence that the utility is being appropriately proactive, or alternately may serve to identify gaps or areas where additional funding may be needed.

APPENDIX G
Selected Acronyms Related to Water Resources and Climate Change

Acronym	Definition	Acronym	Definition
ACWI	Advisory Committee on Water Information	NACC	National Assessment on Climate Change
BLM	Bureau of Land Management	NASA	National Aeronautics and Space Administration
CCAWWG	Climate Change and Water Working Group	NAWQA	National Water Quality Assessment Program
CDC	Centers for Disease Control and Prevention	NCDC	National Climate Data Center
CENRS	Committee on Environment, Natural Resources and Sustainability (OSTP)	NEP	National Estuary Program
CEQ	White House Council on Environmental Quality	NIDIS	National Integrated Drought Information System
CREAT	Climate Resilience Education and Awareness Tool	NOAA	National Oceanic and Atmospheric Administration
CSC	Climate Science Centers	NPS	National Park Service
CUAHSI	Consortium of Universities for the Advancement of Hydrologic Science, Inc.	NPDES	National Pollutant Discharge Elimination System
DOC	United States Department of Commerce	NRC	National Research Council
DOE	United States Department of Energy	NRCS	Natural Resources Conservation Service
DOI	United States Department of the Interior	NSF	National Science Foundation
DOT	United States Department of Transportation	NSTC	National Science and Technology Council
EIA	Energy Information Agency	NWS	National Weather Service
EPA	Environmental Protection Agency	OSTP	Office of Science and Technology Policy
FACA	Federal Advisory Committee Act	RISA	Regional Integrated Sciences and Assessments
FCA	Farm Credit Administration	SBA	Small Business Administration
FERC	Federal Energy Regulatory Commission	SDWA	Safe Drinking Water Act
GCMs	Global Climate Models	SWAQ	Subcommittee on Water Availability and Quality
HIS	Hydrologic Information System	TVA	Tennessee Valley Authority
IBWC	International Boundary and Water Commission	USACE	United States Army Corps of Engineers
ICCATF	Interagency Climate Change Adaptation Task Force	USBR	United States Bureau of Reclamation
ICWP	Interstate Council on Water Policy	USDA	United States Department of Agriculture
IJC	International Joint Commission	USFWS	United States Fish and Wildlife Service
IPCC	Intergovernmental Panel on Climate Change	USGCRP	United States Global Change Research Program
IRS	Internal Revenue Service	USGS	United States Geological Survey
IWRM	Integrated Water Resource Management	USITC	United States International Trade Commission
IWRSS	Integrated Water Resources Science and Services	VATA	Vulnerability Assessment Techniques and Applications
LCC	Landscape Conservation Cooperative	WRCCW	Water Resources and Climate Change Workgroup
		WSTB	Water and Science Technology Board

www.ingramcontent.com/pod-product-compliance
Lightning Source LLC
Chambersburg PA
CBHW081851280526

45789CB00007B/2653